Michael Angelo by Henry Wadsworth Longfellow

Henry Wadsworth Longfellow was born on February 27th, 1807 in Portland, Maine. As a young boy, it was obvious that he was very studious and he quickly became fluent in Latin.

He published his first poem, "The Battle of Lovell's Pond", in the Portland Gazette on November 17th, 1820. He was already thinking of a career in literature and, in his senior year, wrote to his father: "I will not disguise it in the least... the fact is, I most eagerly aspire after future eminence in literature, my whole soul burns most ardently after it, and every earthly thought centers in it...."

After graduation travels in Europe occupied the next three years and he seemed to easily absorb any language he set himself to learn.

On September 14th, 1831, Longfellow married Mary Storer Potter. They settled in Brunswick.

His first published book was in 1833, a translation of poems by the Spanish poet Jorge Manrique. He also published a travel book, Outre-Mer: A Pilgrimage Beyond the Sea.

During a trip to Europe Mary became pregnant. Sadly, in October 1835, she miscarried at some six months. After weeks of illness she died, at the age of 22 on November 29th, 1835. Longfellow wrote "One thought occupies me night and day... She is dead — She is dead! All day I am weary and sad".

In late 1839, Longfellow published Hyperion, a book in prose inspired by his trips abroad.

Ballads and Other Poems was published in 1841 and included "The Village Blacksmith" and "The Wreck of the Hesperus". His reputation as a poet, and a commercial one at that, was set.

On May 10th, 1843, after seven years in pursuit of a chance for new love, Longfellow received word from Fanny Appleton that she agreed to marry him.

On November 1st, 1847, the epic poem Evangeline was published.

In 1854, Longfellow retired from Harvard, to devote himself entirely to writing.

The Song of Haiwatha, perhaps his best known and enjoyed work was published in 1855.

On July 10th, 1861, after suffering horrific burns the previous day. In his attempts to save her Longfellow had also been badly burned and was unable to attend her funeral.

He spent several years translating Dante Alighieri's Divine Comedy. It was published in 1867.

Longfellow was also part of a group who became known as The Fireside Poets which also included William Cullen Bryant, John Greenleaf Whittier, James Russell Lowell, and Oliver Wendell Holmes Snr.

Longfellow was the most popular poet of his day. As a friend once wrote to him, "no other poet was so fully recognized in his lifetime". Some of his works including "Paul Revere's Ride" and "The Song of Haiwatha" may have rewritten the facts but became essential parts of the American psyche and culture.

Henry Wadsworth Longfellow died, surrounded by family, on Friday, March 24th, 1882. He had been suffering from peritonitis.

Index of Contents

MICHAEL ANGELO

Michel, piu che mortal, Angel divino. — ***ARIOSTO.***

DEDICATION

Nothing that is shall perish utterly,
But perish only to revive again
In other forms, as clouds restore in rain

The exhalations of the land and sea.
Men build their houses from the masonry
Of ruined tombs; the passion and the pain
Of hearts, that long have ceased to beat, remain
To throb in hearts that are, or are to be.
So from old chronicles, where sleep in dust
Names that once filled the world with trumpet tones,
I build this verse; and flowers of song have thrust
Their roots among the loose disjointed stones,
Which to this end I fashion as I must.
Quickened are they that touch the Prophet's bones.

I

PROLOGUE AT ISCHIA

The Castle Terrace

VITTORIA COLONNA, and **JULIA GONZAGA**.

VITTORIA
Will you then leave me, Julia, and so soon,
To pace alone this terrace like a ghost?

JULIA
To-morrow, dearest.

VITTORIA
Do not say to-morrow.
A whole month of to-morrows were too soon.
You must not go. You are a part of me.

JULIA
I must return to Fondi.

VITTORIA
The old castle
Needs not your presence. No one waits for you.
Stay one day longer with me. They who go
Feel not the pain of parting; it is they
Who stay behind that suffer. I was thinking
But yesterday how like and how unlike
Have been, and are, our destinies. Your husband,
The good Vespasian, an old man, who seemed

A father to you rather than a husband,
Died in your arms; but mine, in all the flower
And promise of his youth, was taken from me
As by a rushing wind. The breath of battle
Breathed on him, and I saw his face no more,
Save as in dreams it haunts me. As our love
Was for these men, so is our sorrow for them.
Yours a child's sorrow, smiling through its tears;
But mine the grief of an impassioned woman,
Who drank her life up in one draught of love.

JULIA

Behold this locket. This is the white hair
Of my Vespasian. This is the flower-of-love,
This amaranth, and beneath it the device
Non moritura. Thus my heart remains
True to his memory; and the ancient castle,
Where we have lived together, where he died,
Is dear to me as Ischia is to you.

VITTORIA

I did not mean to chide you.

JULIA

Let your heart
Find, if it can, some poor apology
For one who is too young, and feels too keenly
The joy of life, to give up all her days
To sorrow for the dead. While I am true
To the remembrance of the man I loved
And mourn for still, I do not make a show
Of all the grief I feel, nor live secluded
And, like Veronica da Gambara,
Drape my whole house in mourning, and drive forth
In coach of sable drawn by sable horses,
As if I were a corpse. Ah, one to-day
Is worth for me a thousand yesterdays.

VITTORIA

Dear Julia! Friendship has its jealousies
As well as love. Who waits for you at Fondi?

JULIA

A friend of mine and yours; a friend and friar.
You have at Naples your Fra Bernadino;
And I at Fondi have my Fra Bastiano,
The famous artist, who has come from Rome
To paint my portrait. That is not a sin.

VITTORIA
Only a vanity.

JULIA
He painted yours.

VITTORIA
Do not call up to me those days departed
When I was young, and all was bright about me,
And the vicissitudes of life were things
But to be read of in old histories,
Though as pertaining unto me or mine
Impossible. Ah, then I dreamed your dreams,
And now, grown older, I look back and see
They were illusions.

JULIA
Yet without illusions
What would our lives become, what we ourselves?
Dreams or illusions, call them what you will,
They lift us from the commonplace of life
To better things.

VITTORIA
Are there no brighter dreams,
No higher aspirations, than the wish
To please and to be pleased?

JULIA
For you there are;
I am no saint; I feel the world we live in
Comes before that which is to be here after,
And must be dealt with first.

VITTORIA
But in what way?

JULIA
Let the soft wind that wafts to us the odor
Of orange blossoms, let the laughing sea
And the bright sunshine bathing all the world,
Answer the question.

VITTORIA
And for whom is meant
This portrait that you speak of?

JULIA
For my friend
The Cardinal Ippolito.

VITTORIA
For him?

JULIA
Yes, for Ippolito the Magnificent.
'T is always flattering to a woman's pride
To be admired by one whom all admire.

VITTORIA
Ah, Julia, she that makes herself a dove
Is eaten by the hawk. Be on your guard,
He is a Cardinal; and his adoration
Should be elsewhere directed.

JULIA
You forget
The horror of that night, when Barbarossa,
The Moorish corsair, landed on our coast
To seize me for the Sultan Soliman;
How in the dead of night, when all were sleeping,
He scaled the castle wall; how I escaped,
And in my night-dress, mounting a swift steed,
Fled to the mountains, and took refuge there
Among the brigands. Then of all my friends
The Cardinal Ippolito was first
To come with his retainers to my rescue.
Could I refuse the only boon he asked
At such a time, my portrait?

VITTORIA
I have heard
Strange stories of the splendors of his palace,
And how, apparelled like a Spanish Prince,
He rides through Rome with a long retinue
Of Ethiopians and Numidians
And Turks and Tartars, in fantastic dresses,
Making a gallant show. Is this the way
A Cardinal should live?

JULIA
He is so young;
Hardly of age, or little more than that;
Beautiful, generous, fond of arts and letters,
A poet, a musician, and a scholar;

Master of many languages, and a player
On many instruments. In Rome, his palace
Is the asylum of all men distinguished
In art or science, and all Florentines
Escaping from the tyranny of his cousin,
Duke Alessandro.

VITTORIA

I have seen his portrait,
Painted by Titian. You have painted it
In brighter colors.

JULIA

And my Cardinal,
At Itri, in the courtyard of his palace,
Keeps a tame lion!

VITTORIA

And so counterfeits
St. Mark, the Evangelist!

JULIA

Ah, your tame lion
Is Michael Angelo.

VITTORIA

You speak a name
That always thrills me with a noble sound,
As of a trumpet! Michael Angelo!
A lion all men fear and none can tame;
A man that all men honor, and the model
That all should follow; one who works and prays,
For work is prayer, and consecrates his life
To the sublime ideal of his art,
Till art and life are one; a man who holds
Such place in all men's thoughts, that when they speak
Of great things done, or to be done, his name
Is ever on their lips.

JULIA

You too can paint
The portrait of your hero, and in colors
Brighter than Titian's; I might warn you also
Against the dangers that beset your path;
But I forbear.

VITTORIA

If I were made of marble,

Of Fior di Persico or Pavonazzo,
He might admire me: being but flesh and blood,
I am no more to him than other women;
That is, am nothing.

JULIA
Does he ride through Rome
Upon his little mule, as he was wont,
With his slouched hat, and boots of Cordovan,
As when I saw him last?

VITTORIA
Pray do not jest.
I cannot couple with his noble name
A trivial word! Look, how the setting sun
Lights up Castel-a-mare and Sorrento,
And changes Capri to a purple cloud!
And there Vesuvius with its plume of smoke,
And the great city stretched upon the shore
As in a dream!

JULIA
Parthenope the Siren!

VITTORIA
And yon long line of lights, those sunlit windows
Blaze like the torches carried in procession
To do her honor! It is beautiful!

JULIA
I have no heart to feel the beauty of it!
My feet are weary, pacing up and down
These level flags, and wearier still my thoughts
Treading the broken pavement of the Past,
It is too sad. I will go in and rest,
And make me ready for to-morrow's journey.

VITTORIA
I will go with you; for I would not lose
One hour of your dear presence. 'T is enough
Only to be in the same room with you.
I need not speak to you, nor hear you speak;
If I but see you, I am satisfied.

[They go in.

Michael Angelo's Studio

He is at work on the cartoon of the Last Judgment.

MICHAEL ANGELO
Why did the Pope and his ten Cardinals
Come here to lay this heavy task upon me?
Were not the paintings on the Sistine ceiling
Enough for them? They saw the Hebrew leader
Waiting, and clutching his tempestuous beard,
But heeded not. The bones of Julius
Shook in their sepulchre. I heard the sound;
They only heard the sound of their own voices.

Are there no other artists here in Rome
To do this work, that they must needs seek me?
Fra Bastian, my Era Bastian, might have done it;
But he is lost to art. The Papal Seals,
Like leaden weights upon a dead man's eyes,
Press down his lids; and so the burden falls
On Michael Angelo, Chief Architect
And Painter of the Apostolic Palace.
That is the title they cajole me with,
To make me do their work and leave my own;
But having once begun, I turn not back.
Blow, ye bright angels, on your golden trumpets
To the four corners of the earth, and wake
The dead to judgment! Ye recording angels,
Open your books and read? Ye dead awake!
Rise from your graves, drowsy and drugged with death,
As men who suddenly aroused from sleep
Look round amazed, and know not where they are!

In happy hours, when the imagination
Wakes like a wind at midnight, and the soul
Trembles in all its leaves, it is a joy
To be uplifted on its wings, and listen
To the prophetic voices in the air
That call us onward. Then the work we do
Is a delight, and the obedient hand
Never grows weary. But how different is it
En the disconsolate, discouraged hours,
When all the wisdom of the world appears
As trivial as the gossip of a nurse
In a sick-room, and all our work seems useless,

What is it guides my hand, what thoughts possess me,
That I have drawn her face among the angels,
Where she will be hereafter? O sweet dreams,
That through the vacant chambers of my heart
Walk in the silence, as familiar phantoms
Frequent an ancient house, what will ye with me?
'T is said that Emperors write their names in green
When under age, but when of age in purple.
So Love, the greatest Emperor of them all,
Writes his in green at first, but afterwards
In the imperial purple of our blood.
First love or last love,—which of these two passions
Is more omnipotent? Which is more fair,
The star of morning or the evening star?
The sunrise or the sunset of the heart?
The hour when we look forth to the unknown,
And the advancing day consumes the shadows,
Or that when all the landscape of our lives
Lies stretched behind us, and familiar places
Gleam in the distance, and sweet memories
Rise like a tender haze, and magnify
The objects we behold, that soon must vanish?

What matters it to me, whose countenance
Is like the Laocoon's, full of pain; whose forehead
Is a ploughed harvest-field, where three-score years
Have sown in sorrow and have reaped in anguish;
To me, the artisan, to whom all women
Have been as if they were not, or at most
A sudden rush of pigeons in the air,
A flutter of wings, a sound, and then a silence?
I am too old for love; I am too old
To flatter and delude myself with visions
Of never-ending friendship with fair women,
Imaginations, fantasies, illusions,
In which the things that cannot be take shape,
And seem to be, and for the moment are.

[Convent bells ring.

Distant and near and low and loud the bells,
Dominican, Benedictine, and Franciscan,
Jangle and wrangle in their airy towers,
Discordant as the brotherhoods themselves
In their dim cloisters. The descending sun
Seems to caress the city that he loves,
And crowns it with the aureole of a saint.
I will go forth and breathe the air a while.

II

SAN SILVESTRO

A Chapel in the Church of San Silvestra on Monte Cavallo

VITTORIA COLONNA, **CLAUDIO TOLOMMEI**, and **OTHERS**.

VITTORIA
Here let us rest a while, until the crowd
Has left the church. I have already sent
For Michael Angelo to join us here.

MESSER CLAUDIO
After Fra Bernardino's wise discourse
On the Pauline Epistles, certainly
Some words of Michael Angelo on Art
Were not amiss, to bring us back to earth.

MICHAEL ANGELO [At the door]
How like a Saint or Goddess she appears;
Diana or Madonna, which I know not!
In attitude and aspect formed to be
At once the artist's worship and despair!

VITTORIA
Welcome, Maestro. We were waiting for you.

MICHAEL ANGELO
I met your messenger upon the way,
And hastened hither.

VITTORIA
It is kind of you
To come to us, who linger here like gossips
Wasting the afternoon in idle talk.
These are all friends of mine and friends of yours.

MICHAEL ANGELO
If friends of yours, then are they friends of mine.
Pardon me, gentlemen. But when I entered
I saw but the Marchesa.

VITTORIA
Take this seat
Between me and Ser Claudio Tolommei,

Who still maintains that our Italian tongue
Should be called Tuscan. But for that offence
We will not quarrel with him.

MICHAEL ANGELO
Eccellenza—

VITTORIA
Ser Claudio has banished Eccellenza
And all such titles from the Tuscan tongue.

MESSER CLAUDIO
'T is the abuse of them and not the use
I deprecate.

MICHAEL ANGELO
The use or the abuse
It matters not. Let them all go together,
As empty phrases and frivolities,
And common as gold-lace upon the collar
Of an obsequious lackey.

VITTORIA
That may be,
But something of politeness would go with them;
We should lose something of the stately manners
Of the old school.

MESSER CLAUDIO
Undoubtedly.

VITTORIA
But that
Is not what occupies my thoughts at present,
Nor why I sent for you, Messer Michele.
It was to counsel me. His Holiness
Has granted me permission, long desired,
To build a convent in this neighborhood,
Where the old tower is standing, from whose top
Nero looked down upon the burning city.

MICHAEL ANGELO
It is an inspiration!

VITTORIA
I am doubtful
How I shall build; how large to make the convent,
And which way fronting.

MICHAEL ANGELO
Ah, to build, to build!
That is the noblest art of all the arts.
Painting and sculpture are but images,
Are merely shadows cast by outward things
On stone or canvas, having in themselves
No separate existence. Architecture,
Existing in itself, and not in seeming
A something it is not, surpasses them
As substance shadow. Long, long years ago,
Standing one morning near the Baths of Titus,
I saw the statue of Laocoon
Rise from its grave of centuries, like a ghost
Writhing in pain; and as it tore away
The knotted serpents from its limbs, I heard,
Or seemed to hear, the cry of agony
From its white, parted lips. And still I marvel
At the three Rhodian artists, by whose hands
This miracle was wrought. Yet he beholds
Far nobler works who looks upon the ruins
Of temples in the Forum here in Rome.
If God should give me power in my old age
To build for Him a temple half as grand
As those were in their glory, I should count
My age more excellent than youth itself,
And all that I have hitherto accomplished
As only vanity.

VITTORIA
I understand you.
Art is the gift of God, and must be used
Unto His glory. That in art is highest
Which aims at this. When St. Hilarion blessed
The horses of Italicus, they won
The race at Gaza, for his benediction
O'erpowered all magic; and the people shouted
That Christ had conquered Marnas. So that art
Which bears the consecration and the seal
Of holiness upon it will prevail
Over all others. Those few words of yours
Inspire me with new confidence to build.
What think you? The old walls might serve, perhaps,
Some purpose still. The tower can hold the bells.

MICHAEL ANGELO
If strong enough.

VITTORIA
If not, it can be strengthened.

MICHAEL ANGELO
I see no bar nor drawback to this building,
And on our homeward way, if it shall please you,
We may together view the site.

VITTORIA
I thank you.
I did not venture to request so much.

MICHAEL ANGELO
Let us now go to the old walls you spake of,
Vossignoria—

VITTORIA
What, again, Maestro?

MICHAEL ANGELO
Pardon me, Messer Claudio, if once more
I use the ancient courtesies of speech.
I am too old to change.

III

CARDINAL IPPOLITO

A Richly Furnished Apartment in the Palace of Cardinal Ippolito. Night.

JACOPO NARDI, an old man, alone.

NARDI
I am bewildered. These Numidian slaves,
In strange attire; these endless ante-chambers;
This lighted hall, with all its golden splendors,
Pictures, and statues! Can this be the dwelling
Of a disciple of that lowly Man
Who had not where to lay his head? These statues
Are not of Saints; nor is this a Madonna,
This lovely face, that with such tender eyes
Looks down upon me from the painted canvas.
My heart begins to fail me. What can he
Who lives in boundless luxury at Rome
Care for the imperilled liberties of Florence,
Her people, her Republic? Ah, the rich

Feel not the pangs of banishment. All doors
Are open to them, and all hands extended,
The poor alone are outcasts; they who risked
All they possessed for liberty, and lost;
And wander through the world without a friend,
Sick, comfortless, distressed, unknown, uncared for.

[Enter **CARDINAL HIPPOLITO**, in Spanish cloak and slouched hat.

IPPOLITO
I pray you pardon me that I have kept you
Waiting so long alone.

NARDI
I wait to see
The Cardinal.

IPPOLITO
I am the Cardinal.
And you?

NARDI
Jacopo Nardi.

IPPOLITO
You are welcome
I was expecting you. Philippo Strozzi
Had told me of your coming.

NARDI
'T was his son
That brought me to your door.

IPPOLITO
Pray you, be seated.
You seem astonished at the garb I wear,
But at my time of life, and with my habits,
The petticoats of a Cardinal would be—
Troublesome; I could neither ride nor walk,
Nor do a thousand things, if I were dressed
Like an old dowager. It were putting wine
Young as the young Astyanax into goblets
As old as Priam.

NARDI
Oh, your Eminence
Knows best what you should wear.

IPPOLITO

Dear Messer Nardi,
You are no stranger to me. I have read
Your excellent translation of the books
Of Titus Livius, the historian
Of Rome, and model of all historians
That shall come after him. It does you honor;
But greater honor still the love you bear
To Florence, our dear country, and whose annals
I hope your hand will write, in happier days
Than we now see.

NARDI

Your Eminence will pardon
The lateness of the hour.

IPPOLITO

The hours I count not
As a sun-dial; but am like a clock,
That tells the time as well by night as day.
So no excuse. I know what brings you here.
You come to speak of Florence.

NARDI

And her woes.

IPPOLITO

The Duke, my cousin, the black Alessandro,
Whose mother was a Moorish slave, that fed
The sheep upon Lorenzo's farm, still lives
And reigns.

NARDI

Alas, that such a scourge
Should fall on such a city!

IPPOLITO

When he dies,
The Wild Boar in the gardens of Lorenzo,
The beast obscene, should be the monument
Of this bad man.

NARDI

He walks the streets at night
With revellers, insulting honest men.
No house is sacred from his lusts. The convents
Are turned by him to brothels, and the honor
Of women and all ancient pious customs

Are quite forgotten now. The offices
Of the Priori and Gonfalonieri
Have been abolished. All the magistrates
Are now his creatures. Liberty is dead.
The very memory of all honest living
Is wiped away, and even our Tuscan tongue
Corrupted to a Lombard dialect.

IPPOLITO
And worst of all his impious hand has broken
The Martinella,—our great battle bell,
That, sounding through three centuries, has led
The Florentines to victory,—lest its voice
Should waken in their souls some memory
Of far-off times of glory.

NARDI
What a change
Ten little years have made! We all remember
Those better days, when Niccola Capponi,
The Gonfaloniere, from the windows
Of the Old Palace, with the blast of trumpets,
Proclaimed to the inhabitants that Christ
Was chosen King of Florence; and already
Christ is dethroned, and slain, and in his stead
Reigns Lucifer! Alas, alas, for Florence!

IPPOLITO
Lilies with lilies, said Savonarola;
Florence and France! But I say Florence only,
Or only with the Emperor's hand to help us
In sweeping out the rubbish.

NARDI
Little hope
Of help is there from him. He has betrothed
His daughter Margaret to this shameless Duke.
What hope have we from such an Emperor?

IPPOLITO
Baccio Valori and Philippo Strozzi,
Once the Duke's friends and intimates are with us,
And Cardinals Salvati and Ridolfi.
We shall soon see, then, as Valori says,
Whether the Duke can best spare honest men,
Or honest men the Duke.

NARDI

We have determined
To send ambassadors to Spain, and lay
Our griefs before the Emperor, though I fear
More than I hope.

IPPOLITO
The Emperor is busy
With this new war against the Algerines,
And has no time to listen to complaints
From our ambassadors; nor will I trust them,
But go myself. All is in readiness
For my departure, and to-morrow morning
I shall go down to Itri, where I meet
Dante da Castiglione and some others,
Republicans and fugitives from Florence,
And then take ship at Gaeta, and go
To join the Emperor in his new crusade
Against the Turk. I shall have time enough
And opportunity to plead our cause.

NARDI [Rising]
It is an inspiration, and I hail it
As of good omen. May the power that sends it
Bless our beloved country, and restore
Its banished citizens. The soul of Florence
Is now outside its gates. What lies within
Is but a corpse, corrupted and corrupting.
Heaven help us all, I will not tarry longer,
For you have need of rest. Good-night.

IPPOLITO
Good-night.

[Enter **FRA SEBASTIANO**; Turkish **ATTENDANTS**.

IPPOLITO
Fra Bastiano, how your portly presence
Contrasts with that of the spare Florentine
Who has just left me!

FRA SEBASTIANO
As we passed each other,
I saw that he was weeping.

IPPOLITO
Poor old man!

FRA SEBASTIANO

Who is he?

IPPOLITO
Jacopo Nardi. A brave soul;
One of the Fuoruseiti, and the best
And noblest of them all; but he has made me
Sad with his sadness. As I look on you
My heart grows lighter. I behold a man
Who lives in an ideal world, apart
From all the rude collisions of our life,
In a calm atmosphere.

FRA SEBASTIANO
Your Eminence
Is surely jesting. If you knew the life
Of artists as I know it, you might think
Far otherwise.

IPPOLITO
But wherefore should I jest?
The world of art is an ideal world,—
The world I love, and that I fain would live in;
So speak to me of artists and of art,
Of all the painters, sculptors, and musicians
That now illustrate Rome.

FRA SEBASTIANO
Of the musicians,
I know but Goudimel, the brave maestro
And chapel-master of his Holiness,
Who trains the Papal choir.

IPPOLITO
In church this morning,
I listened to a mass of Goudimel,
Divinely chanted. In the Incarnatus,
In lieu of Latin words, the tenor sang
With infinite tenderness, in plain Italian,
A Neapolitan love-song.

FRA SEBASTIANO
You amaze me.
Was it a wanton song?

IPPOLITO
Not a divine one.
I am not over-scrupulous, as you know,
In word or deed, yet such a song as that.

Sung by the tenor of the Papal choir,
And in a Papal mass, seemed out of place;
There's something wrong in it.

FRA SEBASTIANO
There's something wrong
In everything. We cannot make the world
Go right. 'T is not my business to reform
The Papal choir.

IPPOLITO
Nor mine, thank Heaven.
Then tell me of the artists.

FRA SEBASTIANO
Naming one
I name them all; for there is only one.
His name is Messer Michael Angelo.
All art and artists of the present day
Centre in him.

IPPOLITO
You count yourself as nothing!

FRA SEBASTIANO
Or less than nothing, since I am at best
Only a portrait-painter; one who draws
With greater or less skill, as best he may,
The features of a face.

IPPOLITO
And you have had
The honor, nay, the glory, of portraying
Julia Gonzaga! Do you count as nothing
A privilege like that? See there the portrait
Rebuking you with its divine expression.
Are you not penitent? He whose skilful hand
Painted that lovely picture has not right
To vilipend the art of portrait-painting.
But what of Michael Angelo?

FRA SEBASTIANO
But lately
Strolling together down the crowded Corso,
We stopped, well pleased, to see your Eminence
Pass on an Arab steed, a noble creature,
Which Michael Angelo, who is a lover
Of all things beautiful, especially

When they are Arab horses, much admired,
And could not praise enough.

IPPOLITO [To an **ATTENDANT**]
Hassan, to-morrow,
When I am gone, but not till I am gone,—
Be careful about that,—take Barbarossa
To Messer Michael Angelo, the sculptor,
Who lives there at Macello dei Corvi,
Near to the Capitol; and take besides
Some ten mule-loads of provender, and say
Your master sends them to him as a present.

FRA SEBASTIANO
A princely gift. Though Michael Angelo
Refuses presents from his Holiness,
Yours he will not refuse.

IPPOLITO
You think him like
Thymoetes, who received the wooden horse
Into the walls of Troy. That book of Virgil
Have I translated in Italian verse,
And shall, some day, when we have leisure for it,
Be pleased to read you. When I speak of Troy
I am reminded of another town
And of a lovelier Helen, our dear Countess
Julia Gonzaga. You remember, surely,
The adventure with the corsair Barbarossa,
And all that followed?

FRA SEBASTIANO
A most strange adventure;
A tale as marvellous and full of wonder
As any in Boccaccio or Sacchetti;
Almost incredible!

IPPOLITO
Were I a painter
I should not want a better theme than that:
The lovely lady fleeing through the night
In wild disorder; and the brigands' camp
With the red fire-light on their swarthy faces.
Could you not paint it for me?

FRA SEBASTIANO
No, not I.
It is not in my line.

IPPOLITO

Then you shall paint
The portrait of the corsair, when we bring him
A prisoner chained to Naples: for I feel
Something like admiration for a man
Who dared this strange adventure.

FRA SEBASTIANO

I will do it.
But catch the corsair first.

IPPOLITO

You may begin
To-morrow with the sword. Hassan, come hither;
Bring me the Turkish scimitar that hangs
Beneath the picture yonder. Now unsheathe it.
'T is a Damascus blade; you see the inscription
In Arabic: La Allah illa Allah,—
There is no God but God.

FRA SEBASTIANO

How beautiful
In fashion and in finish! It is perfect.
The Arsenal of Venice can not boast
A finer sword.

IPPOLITO

You like it? It is yours.

FRA SEBASTIANO

You do not mean it.

IPPOLITO

I am not a Spaniard,
To say that it is yours and not to mean it.
I have at Itri a whole armory
Full of such weapons. When you paint the portrait
Of Barbarossa, it will be of use.
You have not been rewarded as you should be
For painting the Gonzaga. Throw this bauble
Into the scale, and make the balance equal.
Till then suspend it in your studio;
You artists like such trifles.

FRA SEBASTIANO

I will keep it
In memory of the donor. Many thanks.

IPPOLITO

Fra Bastian, I am growing tired of Rome,
The old dead city, with the old dead people;
Priests everywhere, like shadows on a wall,
And morning, noon, and night the ceaseless sound
Of convent bells. I must be gone from here;
Though Ovid somewhere says that Rome is worthy
To be the dwelling-place of all the Gods,
I must be gone from here. To-morrow morning
I start for Itri, and go thence by sea
To join the Emperor, who is making war
Upon the Algerines; perhaps to sink
Some Turkish galleys, and bring back in chains
The famous corsair. Thus would I avenge
The beautiful Gonzaga.

FRA SEBASTIANO

An achievement
Worthy of Charlemagne, or of Orlando.
Berni and Ariosto both shall add
A canto to their poems, and describe you
As Furioso and Innamorato.
Now I must say good-night.

IPPOLITO

You must not go;
First you shall sup with me. My seneschal
Giovan Andrea dal Borgo a San Sepolcro,—
I like to give the whole sonorous name,
It sounds so like a verse of the Aeneid,—
Has brought me eels fresh from the Lake of Fondi,
And Lucrine oysters cradled in their shells:
These, with red Fondi wine, the Caecu ban
That Horace speaks of, under a hundred keys
Kept safe, until the heir of Posthumus
Shall stain the pavement with it, make a feast
Fit for Lucullus, or Fra Bastian even;
So we will go to supper, and be merry.

FRA SEBASTIANO

Beware! I Remember that Bolsena's eels
And Vernage wine once killed a Pope of Rome!

IPPOLITO

'T was a French Pope; and then so long ago;
Who knows?—perhaps the story is not true.

BORGO DELLE VERGINE AT NAPLES

Room in the Palace of Julia Gonzaga. Night.

JULIA GONZAGA, GIOVANNI VALDESSO

JULIA
Do not go yet.

VALDESSO
The night is far advanced;
I fear to stay too late, and weary you
With these discussions.

JULIA
I have much to say.
I speak to you, Valdesso, with that frankness
Which is the greatest privilege of friendship.—
Speak as I hardly would to my confessor,
Such is my confidence in you.

VALDESSO
Dear Countess
If loyalty to friendship be a claim
Upon your confidence, then I may claim it.

JULIA
Then sit again, and listen unto things
That nearer are to me than life itself.

VALDESSO
In all things I am happy to obey you,
And happiest then when you command me most.

JULIA
Laying aside all useless rhetoric,
That is superfluous between us two,
I come at once unto the point and say,
You know my outward life, my rank and fortune;
Countess of Fondi, Duchess of Trajetto,
A widow rich and flattered, for whose hand
In marriage princes ask, and ask it only
To be rejected. All the world can offer
Lies at my feet. If I remind you of it,

It is not in the way of idle boasting,
But only to the better understanding
Of what comes after.

VALDESSO
God hath given you also
Beauty and intellect; and the signal grace
To lead a spotless life amid temptations,
That others yield to.

JULIA
But the inward life,—
That you know not; 't is known but to myself,
And is to me a mystery and a pain.
A soul disquieted, and ill at ease,
A mind perplexed with doubts and apprehensions,
A heart dissatisfied with all around me,
And with myself, so that sometimes I weep,
Discouraged and disgusted with the world.

VALDESSO
Whene'er we cross a river at a ford,
If we would pass in safety, we must keep
Our eyes fixed steadfast on the shore beyond,
For if we cast them on the flowing stream,
The head swims with it; so if we would cross
The running flood of things here in the world,
Our souls must not look down, but fix their sight
On the firm land beyond.

JULIA
I comprehend you.
You think I am too worldly; that my head
Swims with the giddying whirl of life about me.
Is that your meaning?

VALDESSO
Yes; your meditations
Are more of this world and its vanities
Than of the world to come.

JULIA
Between the two
I am confused.

VALDESSO
Yet have I seen you listen
Enraptured when Fra Bernardino preached

Of faith and hope and charity.

JULIA
I listen,
But only as to music without meaning.
It moves me for the moment, and I think
How beautiful it is to be a saint,
As dear Vittoria is; but I am weak
And wayward, and I soon fall back again
To my old ways, so very easily.
There are too many week-days for one Sunday.

VALDESSO
Then take the Sunday with you through the week,
And sweeten with it all the other days.

JULIA
In part I do so; for to put a stop
To idle tongues, what men might say of me
If I lived all alone here in my palace,
And not from a vocation that I feel
For the monastic life, I now am living
With Sister Caterina at the convent
Of Santa Chiara, and I come here only
On certain days, for my affairs, or visits
Of ceremony, or to be with friends.
For I confess, to live among my friends
Is Paradise to me; my Purgatory
Is living among people I dislike.
And so I pass my life in these two worlds,
This palace and the convent.

VALDESSO
It was then
The fear of man, and not the love of God,
That led you to this step. Why will you not
Give all your heart to God?

JULIA
If God commands it,
Wherefore hath He not made me capable
Of doing for Him what I wish to do
As easily as I could offer Him
This jewel from my hand, this gown I wear,
Or aught else that is mine?

VALDESSO
The hindrance lies

In that original sin, by which all fell.

JULIA
Ah me, I cannot bring my troubled mind
To wish well to that Adam, our first parent,
Who by his sin lost Paradise for us,
And brought such ills upon us.

VALDESSO
We ourselves,
When we commit a sin, lose Paradise,
As much as he did. Let us think of this,
And how we may regain it.

JULIA
Teach me, then,
To harmonize the discord of my life,
And stop the painful jangle of these wires.

VALDESSO
That is a task impossible, until
You tune your heart-strings to a higher key
Than earthly melodies.

JULIA
How shall I do it?
Point out to me the way of this perfection,
And I will follow you; for you have made
My soul enamored with it, and I cannot
Rest satisfied until I find it out.
But lead me privately, so that the world
Hear not my steps; I would not give occasion
For talk among the people.

VALDESSO
Now at last
I understand you fully. Then, what need
Is there for us to beat about the bush?
I know what you desire of me.

JULIA
What rudeness!
If you already know it, why not tell me?

VALDESSO
Because I rather wait for you to ask it
With your own lips.

JULIA

Do me the kindness, then,
To speak without reserve; and with all frankness,
If you divine the truth, will I confess it.

VALDESSO

I am content.

JULIA

Then speak.

VALDESSO

You would be free
From the vexatious thoughts that come and go
Through your imagination, and would have me
Point out some royal road and lady-like
Which you may walk in, and not wound your feet;
You would attain to the divine perfection,
And yet not turn your back upon the world;
You would possess humility within,
But not reveal it in your outward actions;
You would have patience, but without the rude
Occasions that require its exercise;
You would despise the world, but in such fashion
The world should not despise you in return;
Would clothe the soul with all the Christian graces,
Yet not despoil the body of its gauds;
Would feed the soul with spiritual food,
Yet not deprive the body of its feasts;
Would seem angelic in the sight of God,
Yet not too saint-like in the eyes of men;
In short, would lead a holy Christian life
In such a way that even your nearest friend
Would not detect therein one circumstance
To show a change from what it was before.
Have I divined your secret?

JULIA

You have drawn
The portrait of my inner self as truly
As the most skilful painter ever painted
A human face.

VALDESSO

This warrants me in saying
You think you can win heaven by compromise,
And not by verdict.

JULIA

You have often told me
That a bad compromise was better even
Than a good verdict.

VALDESSO

Yes, in suits at law;
Not in religion. With the human soul
There is no compromise. By faith alone
Can man be justified.

JULIA

Hush, dear Valdesso;
That is a heresy. Do not, I pray you,
Proclaim it from the house-top, but preserve it
As something precious, hidden in your heart,
As I, who half believe and tremble at it.

VALDESSO

I must proclaim the truth.

JULIA

Enthusiast!
Why must you? You imperil both yourself
And friends by your imprudence. Pray, be patient.
You have occasion now to show that virtue
Which you lay stress upon. Let us return
To our lost pathway. Show me by what steps
I shall walk in it.
[Convent bells are heard.

VALDESSO

Hark! the convent bells
Are ringing; it is midnight; I must leave you.
And yet I linger. Pardon me, dear Countess,
Since you to-night have made me your confessor,
If I so far may venture, I will warn you
Upon one point.

JULIA

What is it? Speak, I pray you,
For I have no concealments in my conduct;
All is as open as the light of day.
What is it you would warn me of?

VALDESSO

Your friendship
With Cardinal Ippolito.

JULIA

What is there
To cause suspicion or alarm in that,
More than in friendships that I entertain
With you and others? I ne'er sat with him
Alone at night, as I am sitting now
With you, Valdesso.

VALDESSO

Pardon me; the portrait
That Fra Bastiano painted was for him.
Is that quite prudent?

JULIA

That is the same question
Vittoria put to me, when I last saw her.
I make you the same answer. That was not
A pledge of love, but of pure gratitude.
Recall the adventure of that dreadful night
When Barbarossa with two thousand Moors
Landed upon the coast, and in the darkness
Attacked my castle. Then, without delay,
The Cardinal came hurrying down from Rome
To rescue and protect me. Was it wrong
That in an hour like that I did not weigh
Too nicely this or that, but granted him
A boon that pleased him, and that flattered me?

VALDESSO

Only beware lest, in disguise of friendship
Another corsair, worse than Barbarossa,
Steal in and seize the castle, not by storm
But strategy. And now I take my leave.

JULIA

Farewell; but ere you go look forth and see
How night hath hushed the clamor and the stir
Of the tumultuous streets. The cloudless moon
Roofs the whole city as with tiles of silver;
The dim, mysterious sea in silence sleeps;
And straight into the air Vesuvius lifts
His plume of smoke. How beautiful it is!

[**VOICES** in the street.

GIOVAN ANDREA

Poisoned at Itri.

ANOTHER VOICE
Poisoned? Who is poisoned?

GIOVAN ANDREA
The Cardinal Ippolito, my master.
Call it malaria. It was sudden.

[JULIA swoons.

V

VITTORIA COLONNA

A Room in the Torre Argentin

VITTORIA COLONNA and **JULIA GONZAGA**.

VITTORIA
Come to my arms and to my heart once more;
My soul goes out to meet you and embrace you,
For we are of the sisterhood of sorrow.
I know what you have suffered.

JULIA
Name it not.
Let me forget it.

VITTORIA
I will say no more.
Let me look at you. What a joy it is
To see your face, to hear your voice again!
You bring with you a breath as of the morn,
A memory of the far-off happy days
When we were young. When did you come from Fondi?

JULIA
I have not been at Fondi since—

VITTORIA
Ah me!
You need not speak the word; I understand you.

JULIA
I came from Naples by the lovely valley
The Terra di Lavoro.

VITTORIA
And you find me
But just returned from a long journey northward.
I have been staying with that noble woman
Renee of France, the Duchess of Ferrara.

JULIA
Oh, tell me of the Duchess. I have heard
Flaminio speak her praises with such warmth
That I am eager to hear more of her
And of her brilliant court.

VITTORIA
You shall hear all
But first sit down and listen patiently
While I confess myself.

JULIA
What deadly sin
Have you committed?

VITTORIA
Not a sin; a folly
I chid you once at Ischia, when you told me
That brave Fra Bastian was to paint your portrait.

JULIA
Well I remember it.

VITTORIA
Then chide me now,
For I confess to something still more strange.
Old as I am, I have at last consented
To the entreaties and the supplications
Of Michael Angelo—

JULIA
To marry him?

VITTORIA
I pray you, do not jest with me! You now,
Or you should know, that never such a thought
Entered my breast. I am already married.
The Marquis of Pescara is my husband,
And death has not divorced us.

JULIA

Pardon me.
Have I offended you?

VITTORIA
No, but have hurt me.
Unto my buried lord I give myself,
Unto my friend the shadow of myself,
My portrait. It is not from vanity,
But for the love I bear him.

JULIA
I rejoice
To hear these words. Oh, this will be a portrait
Worthy of both of you!

[A knock.

VITTORIA
Hark! He is coming.

JULIA
And shall I go or stay?

VITTORIA
By all means, stay.
The drawing will be better for your presence;
You will enliven me.

JULIA
I shall not speak;
The presence of great men doth take from me
All power of speech. I only gaze at them
In silent wonder, as if they were gods,
Or the inhabitants of some other planet.

[Enter **MICHAEL ANGELO**

VITTORIA
Come in.

MICHAEL ANGELO
I fear my visit is ill-timed;
I interrupt you.

VITTORIA
No; this is a friend
Of yours as well as mine,—the Lady Julia,
The Duchess of Trajetto.

MICHAEL ANGELO [To **JULIA**]
I salute you.
'T is long since I have seen your face, my lady;
Pardon me if I say that having seen it,
One never can forget it.

JULIA
You are kind
To keep me in your memory.

MICHAEL ANGELO
It is
The privilege of age to speak with frankness.
You will not be offended when I say
That never was your beauty more divine.

JULIA
When Michael Angelo condescends to flatter
Or praise me, I am proud, and not offended.

VITTORIA
Now this is gallantry enough for one;
Show me a little.

MICHAEL ANGELO
Ah, my gracious lady,
You know I have not words to speak your praise.
I think of you in silence. You conceal
Your manifold perfections from all eyes,
And make yourself more saint-like day by day.
And day by day men worship you the wore.
But now your hour of martyrdom has come.
You know why I am here.

VITTORIA
Ah yes, I know it,
And meet my fate with fortitude. You find me
Surrounded by the labors of your hands:
The Woman of Samaria at the Well,
The Mater Dolorosa, and the Christ
Upon the Cross, beneath which you have written
Those memorable words of Alighieri,
"Men have forgotten how much blood it costs."

MICHAEL ANGELO
And now I come to add one labor more,
If you will call that labor which is pleasure,

And only pleasure.

VITTORIA
How shall I be seated?

MICHAEL ANGELO [Opening his portfolio]
Just as you are. The light falls well upon you.

VITTORIA
I am ashamed to steal the time from you
That should be given to the Sistine Chapel.
How does that work go on?

MICHAEL ANGELO [Drawing]
But tardily.
Old men work slowly. Brain and hand alike
Are dull and torpid. To die young is best,
And not to be remembered as old men
Tottering about in their decrepitude.

VITTORIA
My dear Maestro! have you, then, forgotten
The story of Sophocles in his old age?

MICHAEL ANGELO
What story is it?

VITTORIA
When his sons accused him,
Before the Areopagus, of dotage,
For all defence, he read there to his Judges
The Tragedy of Oedipus Coloneus,—
The work of his old age.

MICHAEL ANGELO
'T is an illusion
A fabulous story, that will lead old men
Into a thousand follies and conceits.

VITTORIA
So you may show to cavilers your painting
Of the Last Judgment in the Sistine Chapel.

MICHAEL ANGELO
Now you and Lady Julia shall resume
The conversation that I interrupted.

VITTORIA

It was of no great import; nothing more
Nor less than my late visit to Ferrara,
And what I saw there in the ducal palace.
Will it not interrupt you?

MICHAEL ANGELO
Not the least.

VITTORIA
Well, first, then, of Duke Ercole: a man
Cold in his manners, and reserved and silent,
And yet magnificent in all his ways;
Not hospitable unto new ideas,
But from state policy, and certain reasons
Concerning the investiture of the duchy,
A partisan of Rome, and consequently
Intolerant of all the new opinions.

JULIA
I should not like the Duke. These silent men,
Who only look and listen, are like wells
That have no water in them, deep and empty.
How could the daughter of a king of France
Wed such a duke?

MICHAEL ANGELO
The men that women marry
And why they marry them, will always be
A marvel and a mystery to the world.

VITTORIA
And then the Duchess,—how shall I describe her,
Or tell the merits of that happy nature,
Which pleases most when least it thinks of pleasing?
Not beautiful, perhaps, in form and feature,
Yet with an inward beauty, that shines through
Each look and attitude and word and gesture;
A kindly grace of manner and behavior,
A something in her presence and her ways
That makes her beautiful beyond the reach
Of mere external beauty; and in heart
So noble and devoted to the truth,
And so in sympathy with all who strive
After the higher life.

JULIA
She draws me to her
As much as her Duke Ercole repels me.

VITTORIA
Then the devout and honorable women
That grace her court, and make it good to be there;
Francesca Bucyronia, the true-hearted,
Lavinia della Rovere and the Orsini,
The Magdalena and the Cherubina,
And Anne de Parthenai, who sings so sweetly;
All lovely women, full of noble thoughts
And aspirations after noble things.

JULIA
Boccaccio would have envied you such dames.

VITTORIA
No; his Fiammettas and his Philomenas
Are fitter company for Ser Giovanni;
I fear he hardly would have comprehended
The women that I speak of.

MICHAEL ANGELO
Yet he wrote
The story of Griselda. That is something
To set down in his favor.

VITTORIA
With these ladies
Was a young girl, Olympia Morate,
Daughter of Fulvio, the learned scholar,
Famous in all the universities.
A marvellous child, who at the spinning wheel,
And in the daily round of household cares,
Hath learned both Greek and Latin; and is now
A favorite of the Duchess and companion
Of Princess Anne. This beautiful young Sappho
Sometimes recited to us Grecian odes
That she had written, with a voice whose sadness
Thrilled and o'ermastered me, and made me look
Into the future time, and ask myself
What destiny will be hers.

JULIA
A sad one, surely.
Frost kills the flowers that blossom out of season;
And these precocious intellects portend
A life of sorrow or an early death.

VITTORIA

About the court were many learned men;
Chilian Sinapius from beyond the Alps,
And Celio Curione, and Manzolli,
The Duke's physician; and a pale young man,
Charles d'Espeville of Geneva, whom the Duchess
Doth much delight to talk with and to read,
For he hath written a book of Institutes
The Duchess greatly praises, though some call it
The Koran of the heretics.

JULIA
And what poets
Were there to sing you madrigals, and praise
Olympia's eyes and Cherubina's tresses?

VITTORIA
No; for great Ariosto is no more.
The voice that filled those halls with melody
Has long been hushed in death.

JULIA
You should have made
A pilgrimage unto the poet's tomb,
And laid a wreath upon it, for the words
He spake of you.

VITTORIA
And of yourself no less,
And of our master, Michael Angelo.

MICHAEL ANGELO
Of me?

VITTORIA
Have you forgotten that he calls you
Michael, less man than angel, and divine?
You are ungrateful.

MICHAEL ANGELO
A mere play on words.
That adjective he wanted for a rhyme,
To match with Gian Bellino and Urbino.

VITTORIA
Bernardo Tasso is no longer there,
Nor the gay troubadour of Gascony,
Clement Marot, surnamed by flatterers
The Prince of Poets and the Poet of Princes,

Who, being looked upon with much disfavor
By the Duke Ercole, has fled to Venice.

MICHAEL ANGELO
There let him stay with Pietro Aretino,
The Scourge of Princes, also called Divine.
The title is so common in our mouths,
That even the Pifferari of Abruzzi,
Who play their bag-pipes in the streets of Rome
At the Epiphany, will bear it soon,
And will deserve it better than some poets.

VITTORIA
What bee hath stung you?

MICHAEL ANGELO
One that makes no honey;
One that comes buzzing in through every window,
And stabs men with his sting. A bitter thought
Passed through my mind, but it is gone again;
I spake too hastily.

JULIA
I pray you, show me
What you have done.

MICHAEL ANGELO
Not yet; it is not finished.

PART SECOND

I

MONOLOGUE

A Room in Michael Angelo's House

MICHAEL ANGELO
Fled to Viterbo, the old Papal city
Where once an Emperor, humbled in his pride,
Held the Pope's stirrup, as his Holiness
Alighted from his mule! A fugitive
From Cardinal Caraffa's hate, who hurls
His thunders at the house of the Colonna,
With endless bitterness!—Among the nuns
In Santa Catarina's convent hidden,

Herself in soul a nun! And now she chides me
For my too frequent letters, that disturb
Her meditations, and that hinder me
And keep me from my work; now graciously
She thanks me for the crucifix I sent her,
And says that she will keep it: with one hand
Inflicts a wound, and with the other heals it.

[Reading.
"Profoundly I believed that God would grant you
A supernatural faith to paint this Christ;
I wished for that which I now see fulfilled
So marvellously, exceeding all my wishes.
Nor more could be desired, or even so much.
And greatly I rejoice that you have made
The angel on the right so beautiful;
For the Archangel Michael will place you,
You, Michael Angelo, on that new day
Upon the Lord's right hand! And waiting that,
How can I better serve you than to pray
To this sweet Christ for you, and to beseech you
To hold me altogether yours in all things."

Well, I will write less often, or no more,
But wait her coming. No one born in Rome
Can live elsewhere; but he must pine for Rome,
And must return to it. I, who am born
And bred a Tuscan and a Florentine,
Feel the attraction, and I linger here
As if I were a pebble in the pavement
Trodden by priestly feet. This I endure,
Because I breathe in Rome an atmosphere
Heavy with odors of the laurel leaves
That crowned great heroes of the sword and pen,
In ages past. I feel myself exalted
To walk the streets in which a Virgil walked,
Or Trajan rode in triumph; but far more,
And most of all, because the great Colonna
Breathes the same air I breathe, and is to me
An inspiration. Now that she is gone,
Rome is no longer Rome till she return.
This feeling overmasters me. I know not
If it be love, this strong desire to be
Forever in her presence; but I know
That I, who was the friend of solitude,
And ever was best pleased when most alone,
Now weary grow of my own company.
For the first time old age seems lonely to me.

[Opening the Divina Commedia.

I turn for consolation to the leaves
Of the great master of our Tuscan tongue,
Whose words, like colored garnet-shirls in lava,
Betray the heat in which they were engendered.
A mendicant, he ate the bitter bread
Of others, but repaid their meagre gifts
With immortality. In courts of princes
He was a by-word, and in streets of towns
Was mocked by children, like the Hebrew prophet,
Himself a prophet. I too know the cry,
Go up, thou bald head! from a generation
That, wanting reverence, wanteth the best food
The soul can feed on. There's not room enough
For age and youth upon this little planet.
Age must give way. There was not room enough
Even for this great poet. In his song
I hear reverberate the gates of Florence,
Closing upon him, never more to open;
But mingled with the sound are melodies
Celestial from the gates of paradise.
He came, and he is gone. The people knew not
What manner of man was passing by their doors,
Until he passed no more; but in his vision
He saw the torments and beatitudes
Of souls condemned or pardoned, and hath left
Behind him this sublime Apocalypse.

I strive in vain to draw here on the margin
The face of Beatrice. It is not hers,
But the Colonna's. Each hath his ideal,
The image of some woman excellent,
That is his guide. No Grecian art, nor Roman,
Hath yet revealed such loveliness as hers.

II

VITERBO

VITTORIA COLONNA at the convent window.

VITTORIA
Parting with friends is temporary death,
As all death is. We see no more their faces,

Nor hear their voices, save in memory;
But messages of love give us assurance
That we are not forgotten. Who shall say
That from the world of spirits comes no greeting,
No message of remembrance? It may be
The thoughts that visit us, we know not whence,
Sudden as inspiration, are the whispers
Of disembodied spirits, speaking to us
As friends, who wait outside a prison wall,
Through the barred windows speak to those within.

[A pause.

As quiet as the lake that lies beneath me,
As quiet as the tranquil sky above me,
As quiet as a heart that beats no more,
This convent seems. Above, below, all peace!
Silence and solitude, the soul's best friends,
Are with me here, and the tumultuous world
Makes no more noise than the remotest planet.
O gentle spirit, unto the third circle
Of heaven among the blessed souls ascended,
Who, living in the faith and dying for it,
Have gone to their reward, I do not sigh
For thee as being dead, but for myself
That I am still alive. Turn those dear eyes,
Once so benignant to me, upon mine,
That open to their tears such uncontrolled
And such continual issue. Still awhile
Have patience; I will come to thee at last.
A few more goings in and out these doors,
A few more chimings of these convent bells,
A few more prayers, a few more sighs and tears,
And the long agony of this life will end,
And I shall be with thee. If I am wanting
To thy well-being, as thou art to mine,
Have patience; I will come to thee at last.
Ye minds that loiter in these cloister gardens,
Or wander far above the city walls,
Bear unto him this message, that I ever
Or speak or think of him, or weep for him.

By unseen hands uplifted in the light
Of sunset, yonder solitary cloud
Floats, with its white apparel blown abroad,
And wafted up to heaven. It fades away,
And melts into the air. Ah, would that I
Could thus be wafted unto thee, Francesco,

A cloud of white, an incorporeal spirit!

III

MICHAEL ANGELO AND BENVENUTO CELLINI

MICHAEL ANGELO, BENVENUTO CELLINI in gay attire.

BENVENUTO
A good day and good year to the divine
Maestro Michael Angelo, the sculptor!

MICHAEL ANGELO
Welcome, my Benvenuto.

BENVENUTO
That is what
My father said, the first time he beheld
This handsome face. But say farewell, not welcome.
I come to take my leave. I start for Florence
As fast as horse can carry me. I long
To set once more upon its level flags
These feet, made sore by your vile Roman pavements.
Come with me; you are wanted there in Florence.
The Sacristy is not finished.

MICHAEL ANGELO
Speak not of it!
How damp and cold it was! How my bones ached
And my head reeled, when I was working there!
I am too old. I will stay here in Rome,
Where all is old and crumbling, like myself,
To hopeless ruin. All roads lead to Rome.

BENVENUTO
And all lead out of it.

MICHAEL ANGELO
There is a charm,
A certain something in the atmosphere,
That all men feel, and no man can describe.

BENVENUTO
Malaria?

MICHAEL ANGELO

Yes, malaria of the mind,
Out of this tomb of the majestic Past!
The fever to accomplish some great work
That will not let us sleep. I must go on
Until I die.

BENVENUTO
Do you ne'er think of Florence?

MICHAEL ANGELO
Yes; whenever
I think of anything beside my work,
I think of Florence. I remember, too,
The bitter days I passed among the quarries
Of Seravezza and Pietrasanta;
Road-building in the marshes; stupid people,
And cold and rain incessant, and mad gusts
Of mountain wind, like howling dervishes,
That spun and whirled the eddying snow about them
As if it were a garment; aye, vexations
And troubles of all kinds, that ended only
In loss of time and money.

BENVENUTO
True; Maestro,
But that was not in Florence. You should leave
Such work to others. Sweeter memories
Cluster about you, in the pleasant city
Upon the Arno.

MICHAEL ANGELO
In my waking dreams
I see the marvellous dome of Brunelleschi,
Ghiberti's gates of bronze, and Giotto's tower;
And Ghirlandajo's lovely Benci glides
With folded hands amid my troubled thoughts,
A splendid vision! Time rides with the old
At a great pace. As travellers on swift steeds
See the near landscape fly and flow behind them,
While the remoter fields and dim horizons
Go with them, and seem wheeling round to meet them,
So in old age things near us slip away,
And distant things go with as. Pleasantly
Come back to me the days when, as a youth,
I walked with Ghirlandajo in the gardens
Of Medici, and saw the antique statues,
The forms august of gods and godlike men,
And the great world of art revealed itself

To my young eyes. Then all that man hath done
Seemed possible to me. Alas! how little
Of all I dreamed of has my hand achieved!

BENVENUTO
Nay, let the Night and Morning, let Lorenzo
And Julian in the Sacristy at Florence,
Prophets and Sibyls in the Sistine Chapel,
And the Last Judgment answer. Is it finished?

MICHAEL ANGELO
The work is nearly done. But this Last Judgment
Has been the cause of more vexation to me
Than it will be of honor. Ser Biagio,
Master of ceremonies at the Papal court,
A man punctilious and over nice,
Calls it improper; says that those nude forms,
Showing their nakedness in such shameless fashion,
Are better suited to a common bagnio,
Or wayside wine-shop, than a Papal Chapel.
To punish him I painted him as Minos
And leave him there as master of ceremonies
In the Infernal Regions. What would you
Have done to such a man?

BENVENUTO
I would have killed him.
When any one insults me, if I can
I kill him, kill him.

MICHAEL ANGELO
Oh, you gentlemen,
Who dress in silks and velvets, and wear swords,
Are ready with your weapon; and have all
A taste for homicide.

BENVENUTO
I learned that lesson
Under Pope Clement at the siege of Rome,
Some twenty years ago. As I was standing
Upon the ramparts of the Campo Santo
With Alessandro Bene, I beheld
A sea of fog, that covered all the plain,
And hid from us the foe; when suddenly,
A misty figure, like an apparition,
Rose up above the fog, as if on horseback.
At this I aimed my arquebus, and fired.
The figure vanished; and there rose a cry

Out of the darkness, long and fierce and loud,
With imprecations in all languages.
It was the Constable of France, the Bourbon,
That I had slain.

MICHAEL ANGELO
Rome should be grateful to you.

BENVENUTO
But has not been; you shall hear presently.
During the siege I served as bombardier,
There in St. Angelo. His Holiness,
One day, was walking with his Cardinals
On the round bastion, while I stood above
Among my falconets. All thought and feeling,
All skill in art and all desire of fame,
Were swallowed up in the delightful music
Of that artillery. I saw far off,
Within the enemy's trenches on the Prati,
A Spanish cavalier in scarlet cloak;
And firing at him with due aim and range,
I cut the gay Hidalgo in two pieces.
The eyes are dry that wept for him in Spain.
His Holiness, delighted beyond measure
With such display of gunnery, and amazed
To see the man in scarlet cut in two,
Gave me his benediction, and absolved me
From all the homicides I had committed
In service of the Apostolic Church,
Or should commit thereafter. From that day
I have not held in very high esteem
The life of man.

MICHAEL ANGELO
And who absolved Pope Clement?
Now let us speak of Art.

BENVENUTO
Of what you will.

MICHAEL ANGELO
Say, have you seen our friend Fra Bastian lately,
Since by a turn of fortune he became
Friar of the Signet?

BENVENUTO
Faith, a pretty artist
To pass his days in stamping leaden seals

On Papal bulls!

MICHAEL ANGELO
He has grown fat and lazy,
As if the lead clung to him like a sinker.
He paints no more, since he was sent to Fondi
By Cardinal Ippolito to paint
The fair Gonzaga. Ah, you should have seen him
As I did, riding through the city gate,
In his brown hood, attended by four horsemen,
Completely armed, to frighten the banditti.
I think he would have frightened them alone,
For he was rounder than the O of Giotto.

BENVENUTO
He must have looked more like a sack of meal
Than a great painter.

MICHAEL ANGELO
Well, he is not great
But still I like him greatly. Benvenuto
Have faith in nothing but in industry.
Be at it late and early; persevere,
And work right on through censure and applause,
Or else abandon Art.

BENVENUTO
No man works harder
Then I do. I am not a moment idle.

MICHAEL ANGELO
And what have you to show me?

BENVENUTO
This gold ring,
Made for his Holiness,—my latest work,
And I am proud of it. A single diamond
Presented by the Emperor to the Pope.
Targhetta of Venice set and tinted it;
I have reset it, and retinted it
Divinely, as you see. The jewellers
Say I've surpassed Targhetta.

MICHAEL ANGELO
Let me see it.
A pretty jewel.

BENVENUTO

That is not the expression.
Pretty is not a very pretty word
To be applied to such a precious stone,
Given by an Emperor to a Pope, and set
By Benvenuto!

MICHAEL ANGELO
Messer Benvenuto,
I lose all patience with you; for the gifts
That God hath given you are of such a kind,
They should be put to far more noble uses
Than setting diamonds for the Pope of Rome.
You can do greater things.

BENVENUTO
The God who made me
Knows why he made me what I am,—a goldsmith,
A mere artificer.

MICHAEL ANGELO
Oh no; an artist
Richly endowed by nature, but who wraps
His talent in a napkin, and consumes
His life in vanities.

BENVENUTO
Michael Angelo
May say what Benvenuto would not bear
From any other man. He speaks the truth.
I know my life is wasted and consumed
In vanities; but I have better hours
And higher aspirations than you think.
Once, when a prisoner at St. Angelo,
Fasting and praying in the midnight darkness,
In a celestial vision I beheld
A crucifix in the sun, of the same substance
As is the sun itself. And since that hour
There is a splendor round about my head,
That may be seen at sunrise and at sunset
Above my shadow on the grass. And now
I know that I am in the grace of God,
And none henceforth can harm me.

MICHAEL ANGELO
None but one,—
None but yourself, who are your greatest foe.
He that respects himself is safe from others;
He wears a coat of mail that none can pierce.

BENVENUTO
I always wear one.

MICHAEL ANGELO
O incorrigible!
At least, forget not the celestial vision.
Man must have something higher than himself
To think of.

BENVENUTO
That I know full well. Now listen.
I have been sent for into France, where grow
The Lilies that illumine heaven and earth,
And carry in mine equipage the model
Of a most marvellous golden salt-cellar
For the king's table; and here in my brain
A statue of Mars Armipotent for the fountain
Of Fontainebleau, colossal, wonderful.
I go a goldsmith, to return a sculptor.
And so farewell, great Master. Think of me
As one who, in the midst of all his follies,
Had also his ambition, and aspired
To better things.

MICHAEL ANGELO
Do not forget the vision.

[Sitting down again to the Divina Commedia.

Now in what circle of his poem sacred
Would the great Florentine have placed this man?
Whether in Phlegethon, the river of blood,
Or in the fiery belt of Purgatory,
I know not, but most surely not with those
Who walk in leaden cloaks. Though he is one
Whose passions, like a potent alkahest,
Dissolve his better nature, he is not
That despicable thing, a hypocrite;
He doth not cloak his vices, nor deny them.
Come back, my thoughts, from him to Paradise.

IV

FRA SEBASTIANO DEL PIOMBO

MICHAEL ANGELO; FRA SEBASTIANO DEL PIOMBO.

MICHAEL ANGELO [Not turning round]
Who is it?

FRA SEBASTIANO
Wait, for I am out of breath
In climbing your steep stairs.

MICHAEL ANGELO
Ah, my Bastiano,
If you went up and down as many stairs
As I do still, and climbed as many ladders,
It would be better for you. Pray sit down.
Your idle and luxurious way of living
Will one day take your breath away entirely.
And you will never find it.

FRA SEBASTIANO
Well, what then?
That would be better, in my apprehension,
Than falling from a scaffold.

MICHAEL ANGELO
That was nothing
It did not kill me; only lamed me slightly;
I am quite well again.

FRA SEBASTIANO
But why, dear Master,
Why do you live so high up in your house,
When you could live below and have a garden,
As I do?

MICHAEL ANGELO
From this window I can look
On many gardens; o'er the city roofs
See the Campagna and the Alban hills;
And all are mine.

FRA SEBASTIANO
Can you sit down in them,
On summer afternoons, and play the lute
Or sing, or sleep the time away?

MICHAEL ANGELO
I never
Sleep in the day-time; scarcely sleep at night.

I have not time. Did you meet Benvenuto
As you came up the stair?

FRA SEBASTIANO
He ran against me
On the first landing, going at full speed;
Dressed like the Spanish captain in a play,
With his long rapier and his short red cloak.
Why hurry through the world at such a pace?
Life will not be too long.

MICHAEL ANGELO
It is his nature,—
A restless spirit, that consumes itself
With useless agitations. He o'erleaps
The goal he aims at. Patience is a plant
That grows not in all gardens. You are made
Of quite another clay.

FRA SEBASTIANO
And thank God for it.
And now, being somewhat rested, I will tell you
Why I have climbed these formidable stairs.
I have a friend, Francesco Berni, here,
A very charming poet and companion,
Who greatly honors you and all your doings,
And you must sup with us.

MICHAEL ANGELO
Not I, indeed.
I know too well what artists' suppers are.
You must excuse me.

FRA SEBASTIANO
I will not excuse you.
You need repose from your incessant work;
Some recreation, some bright hours of pleasure.

MICHAEL ANGELO
To me, what you and other men call pleasure
Is only pain. Work is my recreation,
The play of faculty; a delight like that
Which a bird feels in flying, or a fish
In darting through the water,—nothing more.
I cannot go. The Sibylline leaves of life
Grow precious now, when only few remain.
I cannot go.

FRA SEBASTIANO
Berni, perhaps, will read
A canto of the Orlando Inamorato.

MICHAEL ANGELO
That is another reason for not going.
If aught is tedious and intolerable,
It is a poet reading his own verses,

FRA SEBASTIANO
Berni thinks somewhat better of your verses
Than you of his. He says that you speak things,
And other poets words. So, pray you, come.

MICHAEL ANGELO
If it were now the Improvisatore,
Luigia Pulci, whom I used to hear
With Benvenuto, in the streets of Florence,
I might be tempted. I was younger then
And singing in the open air was pleasant.

FRA SEBASTIANO
There is a Frenchman here, named Rabelais,
Once a Franciscan friar, and now a doctor,
And secretary to the embassy:
A learned man, who speaks all languages,
And wittiest of men; who wrote a book
Of the Adventures of Gargantua,
So full of strange conceits one roars with laughter
At every page; a jovial boon-companion
And lover of much wine. He too is coming.

MICHAEL ANGELO
Then you will not want me, who am not witty,
And have no sense of mirth, and love not wine.
I should be like a dead man at your banquet.
Why should I seek this Frenchman, Rabelais?
And wherefore go to hear Francesco Berni,
When I have Dante Alighieri here.
The greatest of all poets?

FRA SEBASTIANO
And the dullest;
And only to be read in episodes.
His day is past. Petrarca is our poet.

MICHAEL ANGELO
Petrarca is for women and for lovers

And for those soft Abati, who delight
To wander down long garden walks in summer,
Tinkling their little sonnets all day long,
As lap dogs do their bells.

FRA SEBASTIANO
I love Petrarca.
How sweetly of his absent love he sings
When journeying in the forest of Ardennes!
"I seem to hear her, hearing the boughs and breezes
And leaves and birds lamenting, and the waters
Murmuring flee along the verdant herbage."

MICHAEL ANGELO
Enough. It is all seeming, and no being.
If you would know how a man speaks in earnest,
Read here this passage, where St. Peter thunders
In Paradise against degenerate Popes
And the corruptions of the church, till all
The heaven about him blushes like a sunset.
I beg you to take note of what he says
About the Papal seals, for that concerns
Your office and yourself.

FRA SEBASTIANO [Reading]
Is this the passage?
"Nor I be made the figure of a seal
To privileges venal and mendacious,
Whereat I often redden and flash with fire!"—
That is not poetry.

MICHAEL ANGELO
What is it, then?

FRA SEBASTIANO
Vituperation; gall that might have spirited
From Aretino's pen.

MICHAEL ANGELO
Name not that man!
A profligate, whom your Francesco Berni
Describes as having one foot in the brothel
And the other in the hospital; who lives
By flattering or maligning, as best serves
His purpose at the time. He writes to me
With easy arrogance of my Last Judgment,
In such familiar tone that one would say
The great event already had occurred,

And he was present, and from observation
Informed me how the picture should be painted.

FRA SEBASTIANO
What unassuming, unobtrusive men
These critics are! Now, to have Aretino
Aiming his shafts at you brings back to mind
The Gascon archers in the square of Milan,
Shooting their arrows at Duke Sforza's statue,
By Leonardo, and the foolish rabble
Of envious Florentines, that at your David
Threw stones at night. But Aretino praised you.

MICHAEL ANGELO
His praises were ironical. He knows
How to use words as weapons, and to wound
While seeming to defend. But look, Bastiano,
See how the setting sun lights up that picture!

FRA SEBASTIANO
My portrait of Vittoria Colonna.

MICHAEL ANGELO
It makes her look as she will look hereafter,
When she becomes a saint!

FRA SEBASTIANO
A noble woman!

MICHAEL ANGELO
Ah, these old hands can fashion fairer shapes
In marble, and can paint diviner pictures,
Since I have known her.

FRA SEBASTIANO
And you like this picture.
And yet it is in oil; which you detest.

MICHAEL ANGELO
When that barbarian Jan Van Eyck discovered
The use of oil in painting, he degraded
His art into a handicraft, and made it
Sign-painting, merely, for a country inn
Or wayside wine-shop. 'T is an art for women,
Or for such leisurely and idle people
As you, Fra Bastiano. Nature paints not
In oils, but frescoes the great dome of heaven
With sunset; and the lovely forms of clouds

And flying vapors.

FRA SEBASTIANO
And how soon they fade!
Behold yon line of roofs and belfries painted
Upon the golden background of the sky,
Like a Byzantine picture, or a portrait
Of Cimabue. See how hard the outline,
Sharp-cut and clear, not rounded into shadow.
Yet that is nature.

MICHAEL ANGELO
She is always right.
The picture that approaches sculpture nearest
Is the best picture.

FRA SEBASTIANO
Leonardo thinks
The open air too bright. We ought to paint
As if the sun were shining through a mist.
'T is easier done in oil than in distemper.

MICHAEL ANGELO
Do not revive again the old dispute;
I have an excellent memory for forgetting,
But I still feel the hurt. Wounds are not healed
By the unbending of the bow that made them.

FRA SEBASTIANO
So say Petrarca and the ancient proverb.

MICHAEL ANGELO
But that is past. Now I am angry with you,
Not that you paint in oils, but that grown fat
And indolent, you do not paint at all.

FRA SEBASTIANO
Why should I paint? Why should I toil and sweat,
Who now am rich enough to live at ease,
And take my pleasure?

MICHAEL ANGELO
When Pope Leo died,
He who had been so lavish of the wealth
His predecessors left him, who received
A basket of gold-pieces every morning,
Which every night was empty, left behind
Hardly enough to pay his funeral.

FRA SEBASTIANO

I care for banquets, not for funerals,
As did his Holiness. I have forbidden
All tapers at my burial, and procession
Of priests and friars and monks; and have provided
The cost thereof be given to the poor!

MICHAEL ANGELO

You have done wisely, but of that I speak not.
Ghiberti left behind him wealth and children;
But who to-day would know that he had lived,
If he had never made those gates of bronze
In the old Baptistery,—those gates of bronze,
Worthy to be the gates of Paradise.
His wealth is scattered to the winds; his children
Are long since dead; but those celestial gates
Survive, and keep his name and memory green.

FRA SEBASTIANO

But why should I fatigue myself? I think
That all things it is possible to paint
Have been already painted; and if not,
Why, there are painters in the world at present
Who can accomplish more in two short months
Than I could in two years; so it is well
That some one is contented to do nothing,
And leave the field to others.

MICHAEL ANGELO

O blasphemer!
Not without reason do the people call you
Sebastian del Piombo, for the lead
Of all the Papal bulls is heavy upon you,
And wraps you like a shroud.

FRA SEBASTIANO

Misericordia!
Sharp is the vinegar of sweet wine, and sharp
The words you speak, because the heart within you
Is sweet unto the core.

MICHAEL ANGELO

How changed you are
From the Sebastiano I once knew,
When poor, laborious, emulous to excel,
You strove in rivalry with Badassare
And Raphael Sanzio.

FRA SEBASTIANO

Raphael is dead;
He is but dust and ashes in his grave,
While I am living and enjoying life,
And so am victor. One live Pope is worth
A dozen dead ones.

MICHAEL ANGELO

Raphael is not dead;
He doth but sleep; for how can he be dead
Who lives immortal in the hearts of men?
He only drank the precious wine of youth,
The outbreak of the grapes, before the vintage
Was trodden to bitterness by the feet of men.
The gods have given him sleep. We never were
Nor could be foes, although our followers,
Who are distorted shadows of ourselves,
Have striven to make us so; but each one worked
Unconsciously upon the other's thought;
Both giving and receiving. He perchance
Caught strength from me, and I some greater sweetness
And tenderness from his more gentle nature.
I have but words of praise and admiration
For his great genius; and the world is fairer
That he lived in it.

FRA SEBASTIANO

We at least are friends;
So come with me.

MICHAEL ANGELO

No, no; I am best pleased
When I'm not asked to banquets. I have reached
A time of life when daily walks are shortened,
And even the houses of our dearest friends,
That used to be so near, seem far away.

FRA SEBASTIANO

Then we must sup without you. We shall laugh
At those who toil for fame, and make their lives
A tedious martyrdom, that they may live
A little longer in the mouths of men!
And so, good-night.

MICHAEL ANGELO

Good-night, my Fra Bastiano.

[Returning to his work.

How will men speak of me when I am gone,
When all this colorless, sad life is ended,
And I am dust? They will remember only
The wrinkled forehead, the marred countenance,
The rudeness of my speech, and my rough manners,
And never dream that underneath them all
There was a woman's heart of tenderness.
They will not know the secret of my life,
Locked up in silence, or but vaguely hinted
In uncouth rhymes, that may perchance survive
Some little space in memories of men!
Each one performs his life-work, and then leaves it;
Those that come after him will estimate
His influence on the age in which he lived.

V

PALAZZO BELVEDERE

Titian's studio. A painting of Danae with a curtain before it.

TITIAN, **MICHAEL ANGELO**, and **GIORGIO VASARI**.

MICHAEL ANGELO
So you have left at last your still lagoons,
Your City of Silence floating in the sea,
And come to us in Rome.

TITIAN
I come to learn,
But I have come too late. I should have seen
Rome in my youth, when all my mind was open
To new impressions. Our Vasari here
Leads me about, a blind man, groping darkly
Among the marvels of the past. I touch them,
But do not see them.

MICHAEL ANGELO
There are things in Rome
That one might walk bare-footed here from Venice
But to see once, and then to die content.

TITIAN
I must confess that these majestic ruins

Oppress me with their gloom. I feel as one
Who in the twilight stumbles among tombs,
And cannot read the inscriptions carved upon them.

MICHAEL ANGELO
I felt so once; but I have grown familiar
With desolation, and it has become
No more a pain to me, but a delight.

TITIAN
I could not live here. I must have the sea,
And the sea-mist, with sunshine interwoven
Like cloth of gold; must have beneath my windows
The laughter of the waves, and at my door
Their pattering footsteps, or I am not happy.

MICHAEL ANGELO
Then tell me of your city in the sea,
Paved with red basalt of the Paduan hills.
Tell me of art in Venice. Three great names,
Giorgione, Titian, and the Tintoretto,
Illustrate your Venetian school, and send
A challenge to the world. The first is dead,
But Tintoretto lives.

TITIAN
And paints with fires
Sudden and splendid, as the lightning paints
The cloudy vault of heaven.

GIORGIO
Does he still keep
Above his door the arrogant inscription
That once was painted there,—"The color of Titian,
With the design of Michael Angelo"?

TITIAN
Indeed, I know not. 'T was a foolish boast,
And does no harm to any but himself.
Perhaps he has grown wiser.

MICHAEL ANGELO
When you two
Are gone, who is there that remains behind
To seize the pencil falling from your fingers?

GIORGIO
Oh there are many hands upraised already

To clutch at such a prize, which hardly wait
For death to loose your grasp,—a hundred of them;
Schiavone, Bonifazio, Campagnola,
Moretto, and Moroni; who can count them,
Or measure their ambition?

TITIAN
When we are gone
The generation that comes after us
Will have far other thoughts than ours. Our ruins
Will serve to build their palaces or tombs.
They will possess the world that we think ours,
And fashion it far otherwise.

MICHAEL ANGELO
I hear
Your son Orazio and your nephew Marco
Mentioned with honor.

TITIAN
Ay, brave lads, brave lads.
But time will show. There is a youth in Venice,
One Paul Cagliari, called the Veronese,
Still a mere stripling, but of such rare promise
That we must guard our laurels, or may lose them.

MICHAEL ANGELO
These are good tidings; for I sometimes fear
That, when we die, with us all art will die.
'T is but a fancy. Nature will provide
Others to take our places. I rejoice
To see the young spring forward in the race,
Eager as we were, and as full of hope
And the sublime audacity of youth.

TITIAN
Men die and are forgotten. The great world
Goes on the same. Among the myriads
Of men that live, or have lived, or shall live
What is a single life, or thine or mime,
That we should think all nature would stand still
If we were gone? We must make room for others.

MICHAEL ANGELO
And now, Maestro, pray unveil your picture
Of Danae, of which I hear such praise.

TITIAN [Drawing hack the curtain]

What think you?

MICHAEL ANGELO
That Acrisius did well
To lock such beauty in a brazen tower
And hide it from all eyes.

TITIAN
The model truly
Was beautiful.

MICHAEL ANGELO
And more, that you were present,
And saw the showery Jove from high Olympus
Descend in all his splendor.

TITIAN
From your lips
Such words are full of sweetness.

MICHAEL ANGELO
You have caught
These golden hues from your Venetian sunsets.

TITIAN
Possibly.

MICHAEL ANGELO
Or from sunshine through a shower
On the lagoons, or the broad Adriatic.
Nature reveals herself in all our arts.
The pavements and the palaces of cities
Hint at the nature of the neighboring hills.
Red lavas from the Euganean quarries
Of Padua pave your streets; your palaces
Are the white stones of Istria, and gleam
Reflected in your waters and your pictures.
And thus the works of every artist show
Something of his surroundings and his habits.
The uttermost that can be reached by color
Is here accomplished. Warmth and light and softness
Mingle together. Never yet was flesh
Painted by hand of artist, dead or living,
With such divine perfection.

TITIAN
I am grateful
For so much praise from you, who are a master;

While mostly those who praise and those who blame
Know nothing of the matter, so that mainly
Their censure sounds like praise, their praise like censure.

MICHAEL ANGELO
Wonderful! wonderful! The charm of color
Fascinates me the more that in myself
The gift is wanting. I am not a painter.

GIORGIO
Messer Michele, all the arts are yours,
Not one alone; and therefore I may venture
To put a question to you.

MICHAEL ANGELO
Well, speak on.

GIORGIO
Two nephews of the Cardinal Farnese
Have made me umpire in dispute between them
Which is the greater of the sister arts,
Painting or sculpture. Solve for me the doubt.

MICHAEL ANGELO
Sculpture and painting have a common goal,
And whosoever would attain to it,
Whichever path he take, will find that goal
Equally hard to reach.

GIORGIO
No doubt, no doubt;
But you evade the question.

MICHAEL ANGELO
When I stand
In presence of this picture, I concede
That painting has attained its uttermost;
But in the presence of my sculptured figures
I feel that my conception soars beyond
All limit I have reached.

GIORGIO
You still evade me.

MICHAEL ANGELO
Giorgio Vasari, I have often said
That I account that painting as the best
Which most resembles sculpture. Here before us

We have the proof. Behold those rounded limbs!
How from the canvas they detach themselves,
Till they deceive the eye, and one would say,
It is a statue with a screen behind it!

TITIAN
Signori, pardon me; but all such questions
Seem to me idle.

MICHAEL ANGELO
Idle as the wind.
And now, Maestro, I will say once more
How admirable I esteem your work,
And leave you, without further interruption.

TITIAN
Your friendly visit hath much honored me.

GIORGIO.
Farewell.

MICHAEL ANGELO [To **GIORGIO**, going out]
If the Venetian painters knew
But half as much of drawing as of color,
They would indeed work miracles in art,
And the world see what it hath never seen.

VI

PALAZZO CESARINI

VITTORIA COLONNA, seated in an armchair; **JULIA GONZAGA**, standing near her.

JULIA
It grieves me that I find you still so weak
And suffering.

VITTORIA
No, not suffering; only dying.
Death is the chillness that precedes the dawn;
We shudder for a moment, then awake
In the broad sunshine of the other life.
I am a shadow, merely, and these hands,
These cheeks, these eyes, these tresses that my husband
Once thought so beautiful, and I was proud of
Because he thought them so, are faded quite,—

All beauty gone from them.

JULIA
Ah, no, not that.
Paler you are, but not less beautiful.

VITTORIA
Hand me the mirror. I would fain behold
What change comes o'er our features when we die.
Thank you. And now sit down beside me here
How glad I am that you have come to-day,
Above all other days, and at the hour
When most I need you!

JULIA
Do you ever need me?

VITTORIA
Always, and most of all to-day and now.
Do you remember, Julia, when we walked,
One afternoon, upon the castle terrace
At Ischia, on the day before you left me?

JULIA
Well I remember; but it seems to me
Something unreal, that has never been,—
Something that I have read of in a book,
Or heard of some one else.

VITTORIA
Ten years and more
Have passed since then; and many things have happened
In those ten years, and many friends have died:
Marco Flaminio, whom we all admired
And loved as our Catullus; dear Valldesso,
The noble champion of free thought and speech;
And Cardinal Ippolito, your friend.

JULIA
Oh, do not speak of him! His sudden death
O'ercomes me now, as it o'ercame me then.
Let me forget it; for my memory
Serves me too often as an unkind friend,
And I remember things I would forget,
While I forget the things I would remember.

VITTORIA
Forgive me; I will speak of him no more,

The good Fra Bernardino has departed,
Has fled from Italy, and crossed the Alps,
Fearing Caraffa's wrath, because he taught
That He who made us all without our help
Could also save us without aid of ours.
Renee of France, the Duchess of Ferrara,
That Lily of the Loire, is bowed by winds
That blow from Rome; Olympia Morata
Banished from court because of this new doctrine.
Therefore be cautious. Keep your secret thought
Locked in your breast.

JULIA
I will be very prudent
But speak no more, I pray; it wearies you.

VITTORIA
Yes, I am very weary. Read to me.

JULIA
Most willingly. What shall I read?

VITTORIA
Petrarca's
Triumph of Death. The book lies on the table;
Beside the casket there. Read where you find
The leaf turned down. 'T was there I left off reading.

JULIA [Reads]
"Not as a flame that by some force is spent,
But one that of itself consumeth quite,
Departed hence in peace the soul content,
In fashion of a soft and lucent light
Whose nutriment by slow gradation goes,
Keeping until the end its lustre bright.
Not pale, but whiter than the sheet of snows
That without wind on some fair hill-top lies,
Her weary body seemed to find repose.
Like a sweet slumber in her lovely eyes,
When now the spirit was no longer there,
Was what is dying called by the unwise.
E'en Death itself in her fair face seemed fair"—

Is it of Laura that he here is speaking?—
She doth not answer, yet is not asleep;
Her eyes are full of light and fixed on something
Above her in the air. I can see naught
Except the painted angels on the ceiling.

Vittoria! speak! What is it? Answer me!—
She only smiles, and stretches out her hands.

[The mirror falls and breaks.

VITTORIA
Not disobedient to the heavenly vision!
Pescara! my Pescara!

[Dies.

JULIA
Holy Virgin!
Her body sinks together,—she is dead!

[Kneels and hides her face in **VITTORIA'S** lap.

[Enter **MICHAEL ANGELO**

JULIA
Hush! make no noise.

MICHAEL ANGELO
How is she?

JULIA
Never better.

MICHAEL ANGELO
Then she is dead!

JULIA
Alas! yes, she is dead!
Even death itself in her fair face seems fair.
How wonderful! The light upon her face
Shines from the windows of another world.
Saint only have such faces. Holy Angels!
Bear her like sainted Catherine to her rest!

[Kisses **VITTORIA'S** hand.

PART THIRD

I

MONOLOGUE

Macello de' Corvi. A Room in Michael Angelo's House.

MICHAEL ANGELO, standing before a model of St. Peter's.

MICHAEL ANGELO
Better than thou I cannot, Brunelleschi,
And less than thou I will not! If the thought
Could, like a windlass, lift the ponderous stones
And swing them to their places; if a breath
Could blow this rounded dome into the air,
As if it were a bubble, and these statues
Spring at a signal to their sacred stations,
As sentinels mount guard upon a wall.
Then were my task completed. Now, alas!
Naught am I but a Saint Sebaldus, holding
Upon his hand the model of a church,
As German artists paint him; and what years,
What weary years, must drag themselves along,
Ere this be turned to stone! What hindrances
Must block the way; what idle interferences
Of Cardinals and Canons of St. Peter's,
Who nothing know of art beyond the color
Of cloaks and stockings, nor of any building
Save that of their own fortunes! And what then?
I must then the short-coming of my means
Piece out by stepping forward, as the Spartan
Was told to add a step to his short sword.

[A pause.

And is Fra Bastian dead? Is all that light
Gone out, that sunshine darkened; all that music
And merriment, that used to make our lives
Less melancholy, swallowed up in silence
Like madrigals sung in the street at night
By passing revellers? It is strange indeed
That he should die before me. 'T is against
The laws of nature that the young should die,
And the old live; unless it be that some
Have long been dead who think themselves alive,
Because not buried. Well, what matters it,
Since now that greater light, that was my sun,
Is set, and all is darkness, all is darkness!
Death's lightnings strike to right and left of me,
And, like a ruined wall, the world around me
Crumbles away, and I am left alone.
I have no friends, and want none. My own thoughts

Are now my sole companions,—thoughts of her,
That like a benediction from the skies
Come to me in my solitude and soothe me.
When men are old, the incessant thought of Death
Follows them like their shadow; sits with them
At every meal; sleeps with them when they sleep;
And when they wake already is awake,
And standing by their bedside. Then, what folly
It is in us to make an enemy
Of this importunate follower, not a friend!
To me a friend, and not an enemy,
Has he become since all my friends are dead.

II

VIGNA DI PAPA GIULIO

POPE JULIUS III. seated by the Fountain of Acqua Vergine, surrounded by CARDINALS.

JULIUS
Tell me, why is it ye are discontent,
You, Cardinals Salviati and Marcello,
With Michael Angelo? What has he done,
Or left undone, that ye are set against him?
When one Pope dies, another is soon made;
And I can make a dozen Cardinals,
But cannot make one Michael Angelo.

CARDINAL SALVIATI
Your Holiness, we are not set against him;
We but deplore his incapacity.
He is too old.

JULIUS
You, Cardinal Salviati,
Are an old man. Are you incapable?
'T is the old ox that draws the straightest furrow.

CARDINAL MARCELLO
Your Holiness remembers he was charged
With the repairs upon St. Mary's bridge;
Made cofferdams, and heaped up load on load
Of timber and travertine; and yet for years
The bridge remained unfinished, till we gave it
To Baccio Bigio.

JULIUS

Always Baccio Bigio!
Is there no other architect on earth?
Was it not he that sometime had in charge
The harbor of Ancona.

CARDINAL MARCELLO

Ay, the same.

JULIUS

Then let me tell you that your Baccio Bigio
Did greater damage in a single day
To that fair harbor than the sea had done
Or would do in ten years. And him you think
To put in place of Michael Angelo,
In building the Basilica of St. Peter!
The ass that thinks himself a stag discovers
His error when he comes to leap the ditch.

CARDINAL MARCELLO

He does not build; he but demolishes
The labors of Bramante and San Gallo.

JULIUS

Only to build more grandly.

CARDINAL MARCELLO

But time passes:
Year after year goes by, and yet the work
Is not completed. Michael Angelo
Is a great sculptor, but no architect.
His plans are faulty.

JULIUS

I have seen his model,
And have approved it. But here comes the artist.
Beware of him. He may make Persians of you,
To carry burdens on your backs forever.

SCENE II

The same: **MICHAEL ANGELO**

JULIUS

Come forward, dear Maestro! In these gardens
All ceremonies of our court are banished.

Sit down beside me here.

MICHAEL ANGELO [Sitting down]
How graciously
Your Holiness commiserates old age
And its infirmities!

JULIUS
Say its privileges.
Art I respect. The building of this palace
And laying out these pleasant garden walks
Are my delight, and if I have not asked
Your aid in this, it is that I forbear
To lay new burdens on you at an age
When you need rest. Here I escape from Rome
To be at peace. The tumult of the city
Scarce reaches here.

MICHAEL ANGELO
How beautiful it is,
And quiet almost as a hermitage!

JULIUS
We live as hermits here; and from these heights
O'erlook all Rome and see the yellow Tiber
Cleaving in twain the city, like a sword,
As far below there as St. Mary's bridge.
What think you of that bridge?

MICHAEL ANGELO
I would advise
Your Holiness not to cross it, or not often
It is not safe.

JULIUS
It was repaired of late.

MICHAEL ANGELO
Some morning you will look for it in vain;
It will be gone. The current of the river
Is undermining it.

JULIUS
But you repaired it.

MICHAEL ANGELO
I strengthened all its piers, and paved its road
With travertine. He who came after me

Removed the stone, and sold it, and filled in
The space with gravel.

JULIUS
Cardinal Salviati
And Cardinal Marcello, do you listen?
This is your famous Nanni Baccio Bigio.

MICHAEL ANGELO [Aside]
There is some mystery here. These Cardinals
Stand lowering at me with unfriendly eyes.

JULIUS
Now let us come to what concerns us more
Than bridge or gardens. Some complaints are made
Concerning the Three Chapels in St. Peter's;
Certain supposed defects or imperfections,
You doubtless can explain.

MICHAEL ANGELO
This is no longer
The golden age of art. Men have become
Iconoclasts and critics. They delight not
In what an artist does, but set themselves
To censure what they do not comprehend.
You will not see them bearing a Madonna
Of Cimabue to the church in triumph,
But tearing down the statue of a Pope
To cast it into cannon. Who are they
That bring complaints against me?

JULIUS
Deputies
Of the commissioners; and they complain
Of insufficient light in the Three Chapels.

MICHAEL ANGELO
Your Holiness, the insufficient light
Is somewhere else, and not in the Three Chapels.
Who are the deputies that make complaint?

JULIUS
The Cardinals Salviati and Marcello,
Here present.

MICHAEL ANGELO [Rising]
With permission, Monsignori,
What is it ye complain of?

CARDINAL MARCELLO
We regret
You have departed from Bramante's plan,
And from San Gallo's.

MICHAEL ANGELO
Since the ancient time
No greater architect has lived on earth
Than Lazzari Bramante. His design,
Without confusion, simple, clear, well-lighted.
Merits all praise, and to depart from it
Would be departing from the truth. San Gallo,
Building about with columns, took all light
Out of this plan; left in the choir dark corners
For infinite ribaldries, and lurking places
For rogues and robbers; so that when the church
Was shut at night, not five and twenty men
Could find them out. It was San Gallo, then,
That left the church in darkness, and not I.

CARDINAL MARCELLO
Excuse me; but in each of the Three Chapels
Is but a single window.

MICHAEL ANGELO
Monsignore,
Perhaps you do not know that in the vaulting
Above there are to go three other windows.

CARDINAL SALVIATI
How should we know? You never told us of it.

MICHAEL ANGELO
I neither am obliged, nor will I be,
To tell your Eminence or any other
What I intend or ought to do. Your office
Is to provide the means, and see that thieves
Do not lay hands upon them. The designs
Must all be left to me.

CARDINAL MARCELLO
Sir architect,
You do forget yourself, to speak thus rudely
In presence of his Holiness, and to us
Who are his cardinals.

MICHAEL ANGELO [Putting on his hat]

I do not forget
I am descended from the Counts Canossa,
Linked with the Imperial line, and with Matilda,
Who gave the Church Saint Peter's Patrimony.
I, too, am proud to give unto the Church
The labor of these hands, and what of life
Remains to me. My father Buonarotti
Was Podesta of Chiusi and Caprese.
I am not used to have men speak to me
As if I were a mason, hired to build
A garden wall, and paid on Saturdays
So much an hour.

CARDINAL SALVIATI [Aside]
No wonder that Pope Clement
Never sat down in presence of this man,
Lest he should do the same; and always bade him
Put on his hat, lest he unasked should do it!

MICHAEL ANGELO
If any one could die of grief and shame,
I should. This labor was imposed upon me;
I did not seek it; and if I assumed it,
'T was not for love of fame or love of gain,
But for the love of God. Perhaps old age
Deceived me, or self-interest, or ambition;
I may be doing harm instead of good.
Therefore, I pray your Holiness, release me;
Take off from me the burden of this work;
Let me go back to Florence.

JULIUS
Never, never,
While I am living.

MICHAEL ANGELO
Doth your Holiness
Remember what the Holy Scriptures say
Of the inevitable time, when those
Who look out of the windows shall be darkened,
And the almond-tree shall flourish?

JULIUS
That is in
Ecclesiastes.

MICHAEL ANGELO
And the grasshopper

Shall be a burden, and desire shall fail,
Because man goeth unto his long home.
Vanity of vanities, saith the Preacher; all
Is vanity.

JULIUS
Ah, were to do a thing
As easy as to dream of doing it,
We should not want for artists. But the men
Who carry out in act their great designs
Are few in number; ay, they may be counted
Upon the fingers of this hand. Your place
Is at St. Peter's.

MICHAEL ANGELO
I have had my dream,
And cannot carry out my great conception,
And put it into act.

JULIUS
Then who can do it?
You would but leave it to some Baccio Bigio
To mangle and deface.

MICHAEL ANGELO
Rather than that
I will still bear the burden on my shoulders
A little longer. If your Holiness
Will keep the world in order, and will leave
The building of the church to me, the work
Will go on better for it. Holy Father,
If all the labors that I have endured,
And shall endure, advantage not my soul,
I am but losing time.

JULIUS [Laying his hands on **MICHAEL ANGELO'S** shoulders]
You will be gainer
Both for your soul and body.

MICHAEL ANGELO
Not events
Exasperate me, but the funest conclusions
I draw from these events; the sure decline
Of art, and all the meaning of that word:
All that embellishes and sweetens life,
And lifts it from the level of low cares
Into the purer atmosphere of beauty;
The faith in the Ideal; the inspiration

That made the canons of the church of Seville
Say, "Let us build, so that all men hereafter
Will say that we were madmen." Holy Father,
I beg permission to retire from here.

JULIUS
Go; and my benediction be upon you.

[**MICHAEL ANGELO** goes out.

My Cardinals, this Michael Angelo
Must not be dealt with as a common mason.
He comes of noble blood, and for his crest
Bear two bull's horns; and he has given us proof
That he can toss with them. From this day forth
Unto the end of time, let no man utter
The name of Baccio Bigio in my presence.
All great achievements are the natural fruits
Of a great character. As trees bear not
Their fruits of the same size and quality,
But each one in its kind with equal ease,
So are great deeds as natural to great men
As mean things are to small ones. By his work
We know the master. Let us not perplex him.

III

BINDO ALTOVITI

A Street in Rome

BINDO ALTOVITI, standing at the door of his house.

MICHAEL ANGELO, passing.

BINDO
Good-morning, Messer Michael Angelo!

MICHAEL ANGELO
Good-morning, Messer Bindo Altoviti!

BINDO
What brings you forth so early?

MICHAEL ANGELO
The same reason

That keeps you standing sentinel at your door,—
The air of this delicious summer morning.
What news have you from Florence?

BINDO
Nothing new;
The same old tale of violence and wrong.
Since the disastrous day at Monte Murlo,
When in procession, through San Gallo's gate,
Bareheaded, clothed in rags, on sorry steeds,
Philippo Strozzi and the good Valori
Were led as prisoners down the streets of Florence,
Amid the shouts of an ungrateful people,
Hope is no more, and liberty no more.
Duke Cosimo, the tyrant, reigns supreme.

MICHAEL ANGELO
Florence is dead: her houses are but tombs;
Silence and solitude are in her streets.

BINDO
Ah yes; and often I repeat the words
You wrote upon your statue of the Night,
There in the Sacristy of San Lorenzo:
"Grateful to me is sleep; to be of stone
More grateful, while the wrong and shame endure;
To see not, feel not, is a benediction;
Therefore awake me not; oh, speak in whispers."

MICHAEL ANGELO
Ah, Messer Bindo, the calamities,
The fallen fortunes, and the desolation
Of Florence are to me a tragedy
Deeper than words, and darker than despair.
I, who have worshipped freedom from my cradle,
Have loved her with the passion of a lover,
And clothed her with all lovely attributes
That the imagination can conceive,
Or the heart conjure up, now see her dead,
And trodden in the dust beneath the feet
Of an adventurer! It is a grief
Too great for me to bear in my old age.

BINDO
I say no news from Florence: I am wrong,
For Benvenuto writes that he is coming
To be my guest in Rome.

MICHAEL ANGELO
Those are good tidings.
He hath been many years away from us.

BINDO
Pray you, come in.

MICHAEL ANGELO
I have not time to stay,
And yet I will. I see from here your house
Is filled with works of art. That bust in bronze
Is of yourself. Tell me, who is the master
That works in such an admirable way,
And with such power and feeling?

BINDO
Benvenuto.

MICHAEL ANGELO
Ah? Benvenuto? 'T is a masterpiece!
It pleases me as much, and even more,
Than the antiques about it; and yet they
Are of the best one sees. But you have placed it
By far too high. The light comes from below,
And injures the expression. Were these windows
Above and not beneath it, then indeed
It would maintain its own among these works
Of the old masters, noble as they are.
I will go in and study it more closely.
I always prophesied that Benvenuto,
With all his follies and fantastic ways,
Would show his genius in some work of art
That would amaze the world, and be a challenge
Unto all other artists of his time.

[They go in.

IV

IN THE COLISEUM

MICHAEL ANGELO and **TOMASO DE CAVALIERI**

CAVALIERI
What have you here alone, Messer Michele?

MICHAEL ANGELO
I come to learn.

CAVALIERI
You are already master,
And teach all other men.

MICHAEL ANGELO
Nay, I know nothing;
Not even my own ignorance, as some
Philosopher hath said. I am a schoolboy
Who hath not learned his lesson, and who stands
Ashamed and silent in the awful presence
Of the great master of antiquity
Who built these walls cyclopean.

CAVALIERI
Gaudentius
His name was, I remember. His reward
Was to be thrown alive to the wild beasts
Here where we now are standing.

MICHAEL ANGELO
Idle tales.

CAVALIERI
But you are greater than Gaudentius was,
And your work nobler.

MICHAEL ANGELO
Silence, I beseech you.

CAVALIERI
Tradition says that fifteen thousand men
Were toiling for ten years incessantly
Upon this amphitheatre.

MICHAEL ANGELO
Behold
How wonderful it is! The queen of flowers,
The marble rose of Rome! Its petals torn
By wind and rain of thrice five hundred years;
Its mossy sheath half rent away, and sold
To ornament our palaces and churches,
Or to be trodden under feet of man
Upon the Tiber's bank; yet what remains
Still opening its fair bosom to the sun,
And to the constellations that at night

Hang poised above it like a swarm of bees.

CAVALIERI
The rose of Rome, but not of Paradise;
Not the white rose our Tuscan poet saw,
With saints for petals. When this rose was perfect
Its hundred thousand petals were not Saints,
But senators in their Thessalian caps,
And all the roaring populace of Rome;
And even an Empress and the Vestal Virgins,
Who came to see the gladiators die,
Could not give sweetness to a rose like this.

MICHAEL ANGELO
I spake not of its uses, but its beauty.

CAVALIERI
The sand beneath our feet is saturate
With blood of martyrs; and these rifted stones
Are awful witnesses against a people
Whose pleasure was the pain of dying men.

MICHAEL ANGELO
Tomaso Cavalieri, on my word,
You should have been a preacher, not a painter!
Think you that I approve such cruelties,
Because I marvel at the architects
Who built these walls, and curved these noble arches?
Oh, I am put to shame, when I consider
How mean our work is, when compared with theirs!
Look at these walls about us and above us!
They have been shaken by earthquake; have been made
A fortress, and been battered by long sieges;
The iron clamps, that held the stones together,
Have been wrenched from them; but they stand erect
And firm, as if they had been hewn and hollowed
Out of the solid rock, and were a part
Of the foundations of the world itself.

CAVALIERI
Your work, I say again, is nobler work,
In so far as its end and aim are nobler;
And this is but a ruin, like the rest.
Its vaulted passages are made the caverns
Of robbers, and are haunted by the ghosts
Of murdered men.

MICHAEL ANGELO

A thousand wild flowers bloom
From every chink, and the birds build their nests
Among the ruined arches, and suggest
New thoughts of beauty to the architect,
Now let us climb the broken stairs that lead
Into the corridors above, and study
The marvel and the mystery of that art
In which I am a pupil, not a master.
All things must have an end; the world itself
Must have an end, as in a dream I saw it.
There came a great hand out of heaven, and touched
The earth, and stopped it in its course. The seas
Leaped, a vast cataract, into the abyss;
The forests and the fields slid off, and floated
Like wooded islands in the air. The dead
Were hurled forth from their sepulchres; the living
Were mingled with them, and themselves were dead,—
All being dead; and the fair, shining cities
Dropped out like jewels from a broken crown.
Naught but the core of the great globe remained,
A skeleton of stone. And over it
The wrack of matter drifted like a cloud,
And then recoiled upon itself, and fell
Back on the empty world, that with the weight
Reeled, staggered, righted, and then headlong plunged
Into the darkness, as a ship, when struck
By a great sea, throws off the waves at first
On either side, then settles and goes down
Into the dark abyss, with her dead crew.

CAVALIERI
But the earth does not move.

MICHAEL ANGELO
Who knows? who knowst?
There are great truths that pitch their shining tents
Outside our walls, and though but dimly seen
In the gray dawn, they will be manifest
When the light widens into perfect day.
A certain man, Copernicus by name,
Sometime professor here in Rome, has whispered
It is the earth, and not the sun, that moves.
What I beheld was only in a dream,
Yet dreams sometimes anticipate events,
Being unsubstantial images of things
As yet unseen.

MICHAEL ANGELO, BENVENUTO CELLINI.

MICHAEL ANGELO

So, Benvenuto, you return once more
To the Eternal City. 'T is the centre
To which all gravitates. One finds no rest
Elsewhere than here. There may be other cities
That please us for a while, but Rome alone
Completely satisfies. It becomes to all
A second native land by predilection,
And not by accident of birth alone.

BENVENUTO

I am but just arrived, and am now lodging
With Bindo Altoviti. I have been
To kiss the feet of our most Holy Father,
And now am come in haste to kiss the hands
Of my miraculous Master.

MICHAEL ANGELO

And to find him
Grown very old.

BENVENUTO

You know that precious stones
Never grow old.

MICHAEL ANGELO

Half sunk beneath the horizon,
And yet not gone. Twelve years are a long while.
Tell me of France.

BENVENUTO

It were too long a tale
To tell you all. Suffice in brief to say
The King received me well, and loved me well;
Gave me the annual pension that before me
Our Leonardo had, nor more nor less,
And for my residence the Tour de Nesle,
Upon the river-side.

MICHAEL ANGELO

A princely lodging.

BENVENUTO
What in return I did now matters not,
For there are other things, of greater moment,
I wish to speak of. First of all, the letter
You wrote me, not long since, about my bust
Of Bindo Altoviti, here in Rome. You said,
"My Benvenuto, I for many years
Have known you as the greatest of all goldsmiths,
And now I know you as no less a sculptor."
Ah, generous Master! How shall I e'er thank you
For such kind language?

MICHAEL ANGELO
By believing it.
I saw the bust at Messer Bindo's house,
And thought it worthy of the ancient masters,
And said so. That is all.

BENVENUTO
It is too much;
And I should stand abashed here in your presence,
Had I done nothing worthier of your praise
Than Bindo's bust.

MICHAEL ANGELO
What have you done that's better?

BENVENUTO
When I left Rome for Paris, you remember
I promised you that if I went a goldsmith
I would return a sculptor. I have kept
The promise I then made.

MICHAEL ANGELO
Dear Benvenuto,
I recognized the latent genius in you,
But feared your vices.

BENVENUTO
I have turned them all
To virtues. My impatient, wayward nature,
That made me quick in quarrel, now has served me
Where meekness could not, and where patience could not,
As you shall hear now. I have cast in bronze
A statue of Perseus, holding thus aloft
In his left hand the head of the Medusa,
And in his right the sword that severed it;

His right foot planted on the lifeless corse;
His face superb and pitiful, with eyes
Down-looking on the victim of his vengeance.

MICHAEL ANGELO
I see it as it should be.

BENVENUTO
As it will be
When it is placed upon the Ducal Square,
Half-way between your David and the Judith
Of Donatello.

MICHAEL ANGELO
Rival of them both!

BENVENUTO
But ah, what infinite trouble have I had
With Bandinello, and that stupid beast,
The major-domo of Duke Cosimo,
Francesco Ricci, and their wretched agent
Gorini, who came crawling round about me
Like a black spider, with his whining voice
That sounded like the buzz of a mosquito!
Oh, I have wept in utter desperation,
And wished a thousand times I had not left
My Tour do Nesle, nor e'er returned to Florence,
Or thought of Perseus. What malignant falsehoods
They told the Grand Duke, to impede my work,
And make me desperate!

MICHAEL ANGELO
The nimble lie
Is like the second-hand upon a clock;
We see it fly; while the hour-hand of truth
Seems to stand still, and yet it moves unseen,
And wins at last, for the clock will not strike
Till it has reached the goal.

BENVENUTO
My obstinacy
Stood me in stead, and helped me to o'ercome
The hindrances that envy and ill-will
Put in my way.

MICHAEL ANGELO
When anything is done
People see not the patient doing of it,

Nor think how great would be the loss to man
If it had not been done. As in a building
Stone rests on stone, and wanting the foundation
All would be wanting, so in human life
Each action rests on the foregone event,
That made it possible, but is forgotten
And buried in the earth.

BENVENUTO
Even Bandinello,
Who never yet spake well of anything,
Speaks well of this; and yet he told the Duke
That, though I cast small figures well enough,
I never could cast this.

MICHAEL ANGELO
But you have done it,
And proved Ser Bandinello a false prophet.
That is the wisest way.

BENVENUTO
And ah, that casting
What a wild scene it was, as late at night,
A night of wind and rain, we heaped the furnace
With pine of Serristori, till the flames
Caught in the rafters over us, and threatened
To send the burning roof upon our heads;
And from the garden side the wind and rain
Poured in upon us, and half quenched our fires.
I was beside myself with desperation.
A shudder came upon me, then a fever;
I thought that I was dying, and was forced
To leave the work-shop, and to throw myself
Upon my bed, as one who has no hope.
And as I lay there, a deformed old man
Appeared before me, and with dismal voice,
Like one who doth exhort a criminal
Led forth to death, exclaimed, "Poor Benvenuto,
Thy work is spoiled! There is no remedy!"
Then, with a cry so loud it might have reached
The heaven of fire, I bounded to my feet,
And rushed back to my workmen. They all stood
Bewildered and desponding; and I looked
Into the furnace, and beheld the mass
Half molten only, and in my despair
I fed the fire with oak, whose terrible heat
Soon made the sluggish metal shine and sparkle.
Then followed a bright flash, and an explosion,

As if a thunderbolt had fallen among us.
The covering of the furnace had been rent
Asunder, and the bronze was flowing over;
So that I straightway opened all the sluices
To fill the mould. The metal ran like lava,
Sluggish and heavy; and I sent my workmen
To ransack the whole house, and bring together
My pewter plates and pans, two hundred of them,
And cast them one by one into the furnace
To liquefy the mass, and in a moment
The mould was filled! I fell upon my knees
And thanked the Lord; and then we ate and drank
And went to bed, all hearty and contented.
It was two hours before the break of day.
My fever was quite gone.

MICHAEL ANGELO
A strange adventure,
That could have happened to no man alive
But you, my Benvenuto.

BENVENUTO
As my workmen said
To major-domo Ricci afterward,
When he inquired of them: "'T was not a man,
But an express great devil."

MICHAEL ANGELO
And the statue?

BENVENUTO
Perfect in every part, save the right foot
Of Perseus, as I had foretold the Duke.
There was just bronze enough to fill the mould;
Not a drop over, not a drop too little.
I looked upon it as a miracle
Wrought by the hand of God.

MICHAEL ANGELO
And now I see
How you have turned your vices into virtues.

BENVENUTO
But wherefore do I prate of this? I came
To speak of other things. Duke Cosimo
Through me invites you to return to Florence,
And offers you great honors, even to make you
One of the Forty-Eight, his Senators.

MICHAEL ANGELO

His Senators! That is enough. Since Florence
Was changed by Clement Seventh from a Republic
Into a Dukedom, I no longer wish
To be a Florentine. That dream is ended.
The Grand Duke Cosimo now reigns supreme;
All liberty is dead. Ah, woe is me!
I hoped to see my country rise to heights
Of happiness and freedom yet unreached
By other nations, but the climbing wave
Pauses, lets go its hold, and slides again
Back to the common level, with a hoarse
Death rattle in its throat. I am too old
To hope for better days. I will stay here
And die in Rome. The very weeds, that grow
Among the broken fragments of her ruins,
Are sweeter to me than the garden flowers
Of other cities; and the desolate ring
Of the Campagna round about her walls
Fairer than all the villas that encircle
The towns of Tuscany.

BENVENUTO

But your old friends!

MICHAEL ANGELO

All dead by violence. Baccio Valori
Has been beheaded; Guicciardini poisoned;
Philippo Strozzi strangled in his prison.
Is Florence then a place for honest men
To flourish in? What is there to prevent
My sharing the same fate?

BENVENUTO

Why this: if all
Your friends are dead, so are your enemies.

MICHAEL ANGELO

Is Aretino dead?

BENVENUTO

He lives in Venice,
And not in Florence.

MICHAEL ANGELO

'T is the same to me
This wretched mountebank, whom flatterers

Call the Divine, as if to make the word
Unpleasant in the mouths of those who speak it
And in the ears of those who hear it, sends me
A letter written for the public eye,
And with such subtle and infernal malice,
I wonder at his wickedness. 'T is he
Is the express great devil, and not you.
Some years ago he told me how to paint
The scenes of the Last Judgment.

BENVENUTO
I remember.

MICHAEL ANGELO
Well, now he writes to me that, as a Christian,
He is ashamed of the unbounded freedom
With which I represent it.

BENVENUTO
Hypocrite!

MICHAEL ANGELO
He says I show mankind that I am wanting
In piety and religion, in proportion
As I profess perfection in my art.
Profess perfection? Why, 't is only men
Like Bugiardini who are satisfied
With what they do. I never am content,
But always see the labors of my hand
Fall short of my conception.

BENVENUTO
I perceive
The malice of this creature. He would taint you
With heresy, and in a time like this!
'T is infamous!

MICHAEL ANGELO
I represent the angels
Without their heavenly glory, and the saints
Without a trace of earthly modesty.

BENVENUTO
Incredible audacity!

MICHAEL ANGELO
The heathen
Veiled their Diana with some drapery,

And when they represented Venus naked
They made her by her modest attitude,
Appear half clothed. But I, who am a Christian,
Do so subordinate belief to art
That I have made the very violation
Of modesty in martyrs and in virgins
A spectacle at which all men would gaze
With half-averted eyes even in a brothel.

BENVENUTO
He is at home there, and he ought to know
What men avert their eyes from in such places;
From the Last Judgment chiefly, I imagine.

MICHAEL ANGELO
But divine Providence will never leave
The boldness of my marvellous work unpunished;
And the more marvellous it is, the more
'T is sure to prove the ruin of my fame!
And finally, if in this composition
I had pursued the instructions that he gave me
Concerning heaven and hell and paradise,
In that same letter, known to all the world,
Nature would not be forced, as she is now,
To feel ashamed that she invested me
With such great talent; that I stand myself
A very idol in the world of art.
He taunts me also with the Mausoleum
Of Julius, still unfinished, for the reason
That men persuaded the inane old man
It was of evil augury to build
His tomb while he was living; and he speaks
Of heaps of gold this Pope bequeathed to me,
And calls it robbery;—that is what he says.
What prompted such a letter?

BENVENUTO
Vanity.
He is a clever writer, and he likes
To draw his pen, and flourish it in the face
Of every honest man, as swordsmen do
Their rapiers on occasion, but to show
How skilfully they do it. Had you followed
The advice he gave, or even thanked him for it,
You would have seen another style of fence.
'T is but his wounded vanity, and the wish
To see his name in print. So give it not
A moment's thought; it soon will be forgotten.

MICHAEL ANGELO
I will not think of it, but let it pass
For a rude speech thrown at me in the street,
As boys threw stones at Dante.

BENVENUTO
And what answer
Shall I take back to Grand Duke Cosimo?
He does not ask your labor or your service;
Only your presence in the city of Florence,
With such advice upon his work in hand
As he may ask, and you may choose to give.

MICHAEL ANGELO
You have my answer. Nothing he can offer
Shall tempt me to leave Rome. My work is here,
And only here, the building of St. Peter's.
What other things I hitherto have done
Have fallen from me, are no longer mine;
I have passed on beyond them, and have left them
As milestones on the way. What lies before me,
That is still mine, and while it is unfinished
No one shall draw me from it, or persuade me,
By promises of ease, or wealth, or honor,
Till I behold the finished dome uprise
Complete, as now I see it in my thought.

BENVENUTO
And will you paint no more?

MICHAEL ANGELO
No more.

BENVENUTO
'T is well.
Sculpture is more divine, and more like Nature,
That fashions all her works in high relief,
And that is sculpture. This vast ball, the Earth,
Was moulded out of clay, and baked in fire;
Men, women, and all animals that breathe
Are statues, and not paintings. Even the plants,
The flowers, the fruits, the grasses, were first sculptured,
And colored later. Painting is a lie,
A shadow merely.

MICHAEL ANGELO
Truly, as you say,

Sculpture is more than painting. It is greater
To raise the dead to life than to create
Phantoms that seem to live. The most majestic
Of the three sister arts is that which builds;
The eldest of them all, to whom the others
Are but the hand-maids and the servitors,
Being but imitation, not creation.
Henceforth I dedicate myself to her.

BENVENUTO
And no more from the marble hew those forms
That fill us all with wonder?

MICHAEL ANGELO
Many statues
Will there be room for in my work. Their station
Already is assigned them in my mind.
But things move slowly. There are hindrances,
Want of material, want of means, delays
And interruptions, endless interference
Of Cardinal Commissioners, and disputes
And jealousies of artists, that annoy me.
But twill persevere until the work
Is wholly finished, or till I sink down
Surprised by death, that unexpected guest,
Who waits for no man's leisure, but steps in,
Unasked and unannounced, to put a stop
To all our occupations and designs.
And then perhaps I may go back to Florence;
This is my answer to Duke Cosimo.

VI

MICHAEL ANGELO'S STUDIO

MICHAEL ANGELO and **URBINO.**

MICHAEL ANGELO [Pausing in his work]
Urbino, thou and I are both old men.
My strength begins to fail me.

URBINO
Eccellenza.
That is impossible. Do I not see you
Attack the marble blocks with the same fury
As twenty years ago?

MICHAEL ANGELO
'T is an old habit.
I must have learned it early from my nurse
At Setignano, the stone-mason's wife;
For the first sounds I heard were of the chisel
chipping away the stone.

URBINO
At every stroke
You strike fire with your chisel.

MICHAEL ANGELO
Ay, because
The marble is too hard.

URBINO
It is a block
That Topolino sent you from Carrara.
He is a judge of marble.

MICHAEL ANGELO
I remember.
With it he sent me something of his making,—
A Mercury, with long body and short legs,
As if by any possibility
A messenger of the gods could have short legs.
It was no more like Mercury than you are,
But rather like those little plaster figures
That peddlers hawk about the villages
As images of saints. But luckily
For Topolino, there are many people
Who see no difference between what is best
And what is only good, or not even good;
So that poor artists stand in their esteem
On the same level with the best, or higher.

URBINO
How Eccellenza laughed!

MICHAEL ANGELO
Poor Topolino!
All men are not born artists, nor will labor
E'er make them artists.

URBINO
No, no more
Than Emperors, or Popes, or Cardinals.

One must be chosen for it. I have been
Your color-grinder six and twenty years,
And am not yet an artist.

MICHAEL ANGELO
Some have eyes
That see not; but in every block of marble
I see a statue,—see it as distinctly
As if it stood before me shaped and perfect
In attitude and action. I have only
To hew away the stone walls that imprison
The lovely apparition, and reveal it
To other eyes as mine already see it.
But I grow old and weak. What wilt thou do
When I am dead, Urbino?

URBINO
Eccellenza,
I must then serve another master.

MICHAEL ANGELO
Never!
Bitter is servitude at best. Already
So many years hast thou been serving me;
But rather as a friend than as a servant.
We have grown old together. Dost thou think
So meanly of this Michael Angelo
As to imagine he would let thee serve,
When he is free from service? Take this purse,
Two thousand crowns in gold.

URBINO
Two thousand crowns!

MICHAEL ANGELO
Ay, it will make thee rich. Thou shalt not die
A beggar in a hospital.

URBINO
Oh, Master!

MICHAEL ANGELO
I cannot have them with me on the journey
That I am undertaking. The last garment
That men will make for me will have no pockets.

URBINO [Kissing the hand of **MICHAEL ANGELO**]
My generous master!

MICHAEL ANGELO
Hush!

URBINO
My Providence!

MICHAEL ANGELO
Not a word more. Go now to bed, old man.
Thou hast served Michael Angelo. Remember,
Henceforward thou shalt serve no other master.

VII

THE OAKS OF MONTE LUCA

MICHAEL ANGELO, alone in the woods.

MICHAEL ANGELO
How still it is among these ancient oaks!
Surges and undulations of the air
Uplift the leafy boughs, and let them fall
With scarce a sound. Such sylvan quietudes
Become old age. These huge centennial oaks,
That may have heard in infancy the trumpets
Of Barbarossa's cavalry, deride
Man's brief existence, that with all his strength
He cannot stretch beyond the hundredth year.
This little acorn, turbaned like the Turk,
Which with my foot I spurn, may be an oak
Hereafter, feeding with its bitter mast
The fierce wild boar, and tossing in its arms
The cradled nests of birds, when all the men
That now inhabit this vast universe,
They and their children, and their children's children,
Shall be but dust and mould, and nothing more.
Through openings in the trees I see below me
The valley of Clitumnus, with its farms
And snow-white oxen grazing in the shade
Of the tall poplars on the river's brink.
O Nature, gentle mother, tender nurse!
I who have never loved thee as I ought,
But wasted all my years immured in cities,
And breathed the stifling atmosphere of streets,
Now come to thee for refuge. Here is peace.
Yonder I see the little hermitages

Dotting the mountain side with points of light,
And here St. Julian's convent, like a nest
Of curlews, clinging to some windy cliff.
Beyond the broad, illimitable plain
Down sinks the sun, red as Apollo's quoit,
That, by the envious Zephyr blown aside,
Struck Hyacinthus dead, and stained the earth
With his young blood, that blossomed into flowers.
And now, instead of these fair deities
Dread demons haunt the earth; hermits inhabit
The leafy homes of sylvan Hamadryads;
And jovial friars, rotund and rubicund,
Replace the old Silenus with his ass.

Here underneath these venerable oaks,
Wrinkled and brown and gnarled like them with age,
A brother of the monastery sits,
Lost in his meditations. What may be
The questions that perplex, the hopes that cheer him?
Good-evening, holy father.

MONK

God be with you.

MICHAEL ANGELO

Pardon a stranger if he interrupt
Your meditations.

MONK

It was but a dream,—
The old, old dream, that never will come true;
The dream that all my life I have been dreaming,
And yet is still a dream.

MICHAEL ANGELO

All men have dreams:
I have had mine; but none of them came true;
They were but vanity. Sometimes I think
The happiness of man lies in pursuing,
Not in possessing; for the things possessed
Lose half their value. Tell me of your dream.

MONK

The yearning of my heart, my sole desire,
That like the sheaf of Joseph stands up right,
While all the others bend and bow to it;
The passion that torments me, and that breathes
New meaning into the dead forms of prayer,

Is that with mortal eyes I may behold
The Eternal City.

MICHAEL ANGELO
Rome?

MONK
There is but one;
The rest are merely names. I think of it
As the Celestial City, paved with gold,
And sentinelled with angels.

MICHAEL ANGELO
Would it were.
I have just fled from it. It is beleaguered
By Spanish troops, led by the Duke of Alva.

MONK
But still for me 't is the Celestial City,
And I would see it once before I die.

MICHAEL ANGELO
Each one must bear his cross.

MONK
Were it a cross
That had been laid upon me, I could bear it,
Or fall with it. It is a crucifix;
I am nailed hand and foot, and I am dying!

MICHAEL ANGELO
What would you see in Rome?

MONK
His Holiness.

MICHAEL ANGELO
Him that was once the Cardinal Caraffa?
You would but see a man of fourscore years,
With sunken eyes, burning like carbuncles,
Who sits at table with his friends for hours,
Cursing the Spaniards as a race of Jews
And miscreant Moors. And with what soldiery
Think you he now defends the Eternal City?

MONK
With legions of bright angels.

MICHAEL ANGELO
So he calls them;
And yet in fact these bright angelic legions
Are only German Lutherans.

MONK [Crossing himself]
Heaven protect us?

MICHAEL ANGELO
What further would you see?

MONK
The Cardinals,
Going in their gilt coaches to High Mass.

MICHAEL ANGELO
Men do not go to Paradise in coaches.

MONK
The catacombs, the convents, and the churches;
The ceremonies of the Holy Week
In all their pomp, or, at the Epiphany,
The Feast of the Santissima Bambino
At Ara Coeli. But I shall not see them.

MICHAEL ANGELO
These pompous ceremonies of the Church
Are but an empty show to him who knows
The actors in them. Stay here in your convent,
For he who goes to Rome may see too much.
What would you further?

MONK
I would see the painting
of the Last Judgment in the Sistine Chapel.

MICHAEL ANGELO
The smoke of incense and of altar candles
Has blackened it already.

MONK
Woe is me!
Then I would hear Allegri's Miserere,
Sung by the Papal choir.

MICHAEL ANGELO
A dismal dirge!
I am an old, old man, and I have lived

In Rome for thirty years and more, and know
The jarring of the wheels of that great world,
Its jealousies, its discords, and its strife.
Therefore I say to you, remain content
Here in your convent, here among your woods,
Where only there is peace. Go not to Rome.
There was of old a monk of Wittenberg
Who went to Rome; you may have heard of him;
His name was Luther; and you know what followed.

[The convent bell rings.

MONK [Rising]
It is the convent bell; it rings for vespers.
Let us go in; we both will pray for peace.

VIII

THE DEAD CHRIST

Michael Angelo's Studio.

MICHAEL ANGELO, with a light, working upon the Dead Christ. Midnight.

MICHAEL ANGELO
O Death, why is it I cannot portray
Thy form and features? Do I stand too near thee?
Or dost thou hold my hand, and draw me back,
As being thy disciple, not thy master?
Let him who knows not what old age is like
Have patience till it comes, and he will know.
I once had skill to fashion Life and Death
And Sleep, which is the counterfeit of Death;
And I remember what Giovanni Strozzi
Wrote underneath my statue of the Night
In San Lorenzo, ah, so long ago!

Grateful to me is sleep! More grateful now
Than it was then; for all my friends are dead;
And she is dead, the noblest of them all.
I saw her face, when the great sculptor Death,
Whom men should call Divine, had at a blow
Stricken her into marble; and I kissed
Her cold white hand. What was it held me back
From kissing her fair forehead, and those lips,
Those dead, dumb lips? Grateful to me is sleep!

[Enter **GIORGIO VASARI**.

GIORGIO
Good-evening, or good-morning, for I know not
Which of the two it is.

MICHAEL ANGELO
How came you in?

GIORGIO
Why, by the door, as all men do.

MICHAEL ANGELO
Ascanio
Must have forgotten to bolt it.

GIORGIO
Probably.
Am I a spirit, or so like a spirit,
That I could slip through bolted door or window?
As I was passing down the street, I saw
A glimmer of light, and heard the well-known chink
Of chisel upon marble. So I entered,
To see what keeps you from your bed so late.

MICHAEL ANGELO [Coming forward with the lamp]
You have been revelling with your boon companions,
Giorgio Vasari, and you come to me
At an untimely hour.

GIORGIO
The Pope hath sent me.
His Holiness desires to see again
The drawing you once showed him of the dome
Of the Basilica.

MICHAEL ANGELO
We will look for it.

GIORGIO
What is the marble group that glimmers there
Behind you?

MICHAEL ANGELO
Nothing, and yet everything,—
As one may take it. It is my own tomb,
That I am building.

GIORGIO
Do not hide it from me.
By our long friendship and the love I bear you,
Refuse me not!

MICHAEL ANGELO [Letting fall the lamp]
Life hath become to me
An empty theatre,—its lights extinguished,
The music silent, and the actors gone;
And I alone sit musing on the scenes
That once have been. I am so old that Death
Oft plucks me by the cloak, to come with him
And some day, like this lamp, shall I fall down,
And my last spark of life will be extinguished.
Ah me! ah me! what darkness of despair!
So near to death, and yet so far from God!

Henry Wadsworth Longfellow – A Short Biography

Henry Wadsworth Longfellow was born on February 27th, 1807 in Portland, Maine (then part of Massachusetts) to Stephen Longfellow and Zilpah (nee Wadsworth) Longfellow. His father was a lawyer, and his maternal grandfather, Peleg Wadsworth, was a general in the American Revolutionary War and a Member of Congress.

It was a large family. Longfellow was the second of eight children; his siblings were Stephen (1805), Elizabeth (1808), Anne (1810), Alexander (1814), Mary (1816), Ellen (1818) and Samuel (1819).

Longfellow attended a dame school at the age of three and by age six was enrolled at the private Portland Academy. He was very studious and quickly became fluent in Latin. His mother encouraged his love of reading and learning and introduced him to many literary classics.

He published his first poem, a patriotic four-stanza affair entitled "The Battle of Lovell's Pond", in the Portland Gazette on November 17, 1820. He remained at the Portland Academy until he was fourteen. As a child, he spent much of his summers at his grandfather Peleg's farm in the nearby town of Hiram.

In the fall of 1822, the 15-year-old Longfellow enrolled at Bowdoin College in Brunswick, Maine. His grandfather was a founder of the college and his father a trustee. Here he met and befriended Nathaniel Hawthorne. Longfellow was already thinking of a career in literature. In his senior year he wrote to his father: "I will not disguise it in the least... the fact is, I most eagerly aspire after future eminence in literature, my whole soul burns most ardently after it, and every earthly thought centers in it... I am almost confident in believing, that if I can ever rise in the world it must be by the exercise of my talents in the wide field of literature."

Poetry was the writing form he felt most at ease with and he offered poems to many newspapers and magazines. Between January 1824 and graduation in 1825, he had almost 40 poems published, over half of which were in the short-lived Boston periodical The United States Literary Gazette.

When Longfellow graduated, he was ranked a pleasing fourth in the class, and had been elected to Phi Beta Kappa. He was quickly offered the post of professor of modern languages at his alma mater.

Accounts suggest that part of the requirement of acceptance was to tour Europe to become more immersed in both languages and cultures. Longfellow began his tour of Europe in May 1826 aboard the ship Cadmus. His travels in Europe would last three years and cost his father the princely sum of $2,604.24. He visited France, Spain, Italy, Germany and England before returning to the United States in mid-August 1829.

His stock of languages now included French, Spanish, Portuguese, and German, and impressively, mostly without any formal instruction.

On August 27th, 1829, he wrote to the president of Bowdoin that he was turning down the professorship because he considered the $600 salary "disproportionate to the duties required". The trustees countered by raising the salary to $800 and an additional $100 to serve as the college's librarian, a post which required only one hour's attention a day.

On September 14th, 1831, Longfellow married Mary Storer Potter, a childhood friend from Portland. The couple settled in Brunswick. Longfellow now published several non-fiction and fiction prose pieces inspired by his friend Washington Irving, whom he had met in Madrid during his travels, these included "The Indian Summer" and "The Bald Eagle" in 1833.

During his years teaching at the college, he translated textbooks in French, Italian and Spanish; his first published book was in 1833, a translation of the poetry of the medieval Spanish poet Jorge Manrique. A travel book, Outre-Mer: A Pilgrimage Beyond the Sea, was first published in serial form before a book edition in 1835.

In December 1834, Longfellow received a letter from Josiah Quincy III, president of Harvard College, offering him the Smith Professorship of Modern Languages with the condition that he first spend a year or so abroad. The Longfellow's set off for Europe. He would now be able to add German, Dutch, Danish, Swedish, Finnish, and Icelandic to his repertoire of languages.

During the trip they discovered that Mary was pregnant. Sadly, in October 1835, she miscarried some six months into the pregnancy. Then followed several weeks of illness and at the age of 22 on November 29th, 1835 she died. Longfellow had her body embalmed, placed in a lead coffin itself inside an oak coffin which was then shipped to Mount Auburn Cemetery near Boston. He wrote movingly "One thought occupies me night and day... She is dead—She is dead! All day I am weary and sad".

Back in the United States, Longfellow took up the professorship at Harvard. He was required to live in Cambridge, close to the campus and rented rooms at the Craigie House in the spring of 1837. The home, built in 1759, had once been the headquarters of George Washington during the Siege of Boston.

Longfellow now felt able to publish again, starting with the collection Voices of the Night in 1839. It was mainly comprised of translations together with nine original poems and seven poems written back in his teenage years.

His romantic interests also began to surface again. He had begun to court Frances 'Fanny' Appleton, daughter of the Boston industrialist Nathan Appleton. At first, the independent-minded Appleton was not interested in marriage but Longfellow was determined. In July 1839, he wrote to a friend: "Victory hangs doubtful. The lady says she will not! I say she shall! It is not pride, but the madness of passion".

In late 1839, Longfellow published Hyperion, a book in prose inspired by his trips abroad and his still un-successful courtship of Fanny Appleton. Amidst this, Longfellow fell into "periods of neurotic depression with moments of panic" and required a six-month leave of absence from Harvard to attend a health spa in the former Marienberg Benedictine Convent at Boppard in Germany.

Ballads and Other Poems was published in 1841 and included "The Village Blacksmith" and "The Wreck of the Hesperus". His reputation as a poet, and a commercial one at that, was set.

Longfellow published a play in 1842, The Spanish Student, based on his memories from his time in Spain in the 1820s. A small collection, Poems on Slavery, was also published in 1842. This was Longfellow's first public support of abolitionism. However, as Longfellow himself said, the poems were "so mild that even a Slaveholder might read them without losing his appetite for breakfast". The New England Anti-Slavery Association, however, was satisfied enough with the intent of the collection to reprint it for their own distribution.

On May 10th, 1843, after seven years in pursuit, Longfellow received a letter from Fanny Appleton agreeing to marry him. He was elated and immediately walked 90 minutes to meet her at her house.

Nathan Appleton bought the Craigie House as a wedding present to the pair. Longfellow lived there for the rest of his life. His love for Fanny is evident from Longfellow's only love poem, the sonnet "The Evening Star", written in October 1845:

"O my beloved, my sweet Hesperus!
My morning and my evening star of love!"

He once attended a ball without her and said, "The lights seemed dimmer, the music sadder, the flowers fewer, and the women less fair."

Longfellow and Fanny had six children: Charles Appleton (1844), Ernest Wadsworth (1845), Fanny (1847, who died in infancy), Alice Mary (1850), Edith (1853), and Anne Allegra (1855).

Aware of his growing stature and his ability to influence others he also encouraged and supported many other translators. In 1845, he published The Poets and Poetry of Europe, a large 800-page compendium of translated works by other writers. Longfellow intended the anthology "to bring together, into a compact and convenient form, as large an amount as possible of those English translations which are scattered through many volumes, and are not accessible to the general reader".

On November 1st, 1847, the epic poem Evangeline was published.

Longfellow's literary income was now becoming quite substantial: in 1840, he had made $219 but by 1850 it had grown to a very promising $1,900.

On June 14th, 1853, Longfellow held a farewell dinner party at his Cambridge home for his great friend Nathaniel Hawthorne, who was preparing to move overseas.

In 1854, Longfellow retired from Harvard, devoting himself entirely to writing. He would be awarded an honorary doctorate of laws from Harvard in 1859.

The Song of Haiwatha, his epic poem, and perhaps his best known and enjoyed work was published in 1855.

On a hot July 9th day, 1861, Fanny was putting several locks of her children's hair into an envelope and making attempts to seal it with hot sealing wax while Longfellow took a nap. The circumstances of what happened next vary but the actuality is that Fanny's dress caught fire. Her screams awakened Longfellow who rushed to help her and threw a rug over her and stifled the flames with his own body as best he could, but Fanny was already horrifically burned.

A doctor was called and Fanny was taken to her room to recover. She was in and out of consciousness throughout the night and was also administered ether. The next morning, July 10th, 1861, she died shortly after 10 o'clock after asking for a cup of coffee.

Longfellow, in his effort to save her had also been badly burned and was unable to attend her funeral. His facial injuries required he stopped shaving. The ensuing beard now became the quintessential look that everyone remembers from pictures.

Devastated, he never fully recovered and sometimes resorted to laudanum and ether to ease the pain. He worried he would go insane and begged "not to be sent to an asylum" and noted that he was "inwardly bleeding to death". In the sonnet "The Cross of Snow" (1879), which he wrote eighteen years later he wrote:

"Such is the cross I wear upon my breast
These eighteen years, through all the changing scenes
And seasons, changeless since the day she died".

Longfellow spent several years translating Dante Alighieri's epic poem, The Divine Comedy. To aid him in perfecting the translation and reviewing proofs, he invited several friends to weekly meetings every Wednesday from 1864. This became known as the "Dante Club", and regulars included William Dean Howells, James Russell Lowell, Charles Eliot Norton and other occasional guests. The full three-volume translation was published in the spring of 1867, though Longfellow would continue to revise it. It was wildly popular and was re-printed four times in its first year.

By 1868, Longfellow's annual income was over a staggering $48,000.

Longfellow was also part of a group of Poets who became known as The Fireside Poets. The group included Longfellow, William Cullen Bryant, John Greenleaf Whittier, James Russell Lowell, and Oliver Wendell Holmes Snr. Occasionally Ralph Waldo Emerson is also placed among their number. The name "Fireside Poets" derives from poetry reading as a collective family entertainment of the times.

During the 1860s, Longfellow, still a committed abolitionist, also hoped for a coming together, a reconciliation, between the north and south after the dark days of the Civil War. When his son was wounded during the war, he wrote the poem "Christmas Bells", later the basis of the carol I Heard the Bells on Christmas Day.

In 1874, Samuel Cutler Ward helped him sell the poem "The Hanging of the Crane" to the New York Ledger for $3,000; it was the highest price ever paid for a poem. An astonishing sum. But Longfellow was worth it. His fame and audience were widespread and devoted.

Continuing in his hopes for a better and more united America he wrote in his journal in 1878: "I have only one desire; and that is for harmony, and a frank and honest understanding between North and South". Longfellow, despite his aversion to public speaking, took up an offer from Joshua Chamberlain to speak at his fiftieth reunion at Bowdoin College. Here he read the poem "Morituri Salutamus" so quietly that few could hear.

On August 22th, 1879, a female admirer who seemed to know little about his history, traveled to Longfellow's house in Cambridge and, unaware to whom she was speaking, asked Longfellow: "Is this the house where Longfellow was born?" Longfellow told her it was not. The visitor then asked if he had died here. "Not yet", he replied.

Much of Longfellow's work is recognized for its melody-like musicality. As he says, "what a writer asks of his reader is not so much to like as to listen".

Longfellow, like many others of the period, called for the development of high quality American literature. In his work, Kavanagh, a character says: "We want a national literature commensurate with our mountains and rivers... We want a national epic that shall correspond to the size of the country... We want a national drama in which scope shall be given to our gigantic ideas and to the unparalleled activity of our people... In a word, we want a national literature altogether shaggy and unshorn, that shall shake the earth, like a herd of buffaloes thundering over the prairies."

As a translator Longfellow was very impressive. His translation of Dante's The Divine Comedy became a requirement for those who wanted to be a part of high culture.

In 1874, Longfellow oversaw a 31-volume anthology called Poems of Places, collecting poems of several geographical locations; Europe, Asia, and the Arabian countries. It was a work of great educational endeavor but Emerson was disappointed and is said to have told Longfellow: "The world is expecting better things of you than this... You are wasting time that should be bestowed upon original production".

At this point in his life Longfellow could look back and see that his early collections, Voices of the Night and Ballads and Other Poems, had made him instantly popular. The New-Yorker called him "one of the very few in our time who has successfully aimed in putting poetry to its best and sweetest uses". The Southern Literary Messenger immediately put Longfellow "among the first of our American poets".

The rapidity with which American readers embraced Longfellow was unparalleled in publishing history in the United States. His popularity spread throughout Europe, his poems translated into Italian, French, German, and other languages.

Longfellow was the most popular poet of his day. As a friend once wrote to him, "no other poet was so fully recognized in his lifetime". Some of his works including "Paul Revere's Ride" and "The Song of Haiwatha" may have rewritten the facts but became essential parts of the American psyche and culture. He was so admired that on his 70th birthday in 1877 the atmosphere was that of a national holiday, with parades, speeches, and, of course, the reading of his poems.

Over the years, Longfellow's reputation came to include his personality; he was a gentle, placid, poetic soul. James Russell Lowell said, Longfellow had an "absolute sweetness, simplicity, and modesty". The reality was that Longfellow's life was much more difficult than was assumed. He suffered from neuralgia, which caused him constant pain, and poor eyesight. The difficulties of coping with the loss of two wives also took its toll. He was very quiet, reserved, and private; in later years, he became increasingly unsocial and avoided leaving home if he could.

In March 1882, Longfellow went to bed with severe stomach pain. He endured the pain for several days with the help of opium.

Henry Wadsworth Longfellow died, surrounded by family, on Friday, March 24th, 1882. He had been suffering from peritonitis.

He is buried with both of his wives at Mount Auburn Cemetery in Cambridge, Massachusetts. At Longfellow's funeral, his friend Ralph Waldo Emerson called him "a sweet and beautiful soul".

At the time of his death, his estate was valued at $356,320.

In 1884, Longfellow became the first non-British writer for whom a sculpted bust was placed in Poet's Corner of Westminster Abbey in London; he remains the sole American poet thus represented.

Henry Wadsworth Longfellow – A Concise Bibliography

Outre-Mer: A Pilgrimage Beyond the Sea (Travelogue) (1835)
Hyperion, a Romance (1839)
The Spanish Student. A Play in Three Acts (1843)
Evangeline: A Tale of Acadie (poem) (1847)
Kavanagh (1849)
The Golden Legend (poem) (1851)
The Song of Hiawatha (poem) (1855)
The New England Tragedies (1868)
The Divine Tragedy (1871)
Christus: A Mystery (1872)
Aftermath (poem) (1873)
The Arrow and the Song (poem)

Poetry Collections

Voices of the Night (1839)
Ballads & Other Poems (1841)
Poems on Slavery (1842)
The Belfry of Bruges & Other Poems (1845)
The Seaside and the Fireside (1850)
The Poetical Works of Henry Wadsworth Longfellow (1852)
The Courtship of Miles Standish & Other Poems (1858)
Tales of a Wayside Inn (1863)
Birds of Passage (1863)
Household Poems (1865)
Flower-de-Luce (1867)
Three Books of Song (1872)
The Masque of Pandora & Other Poems (1875)
Kéramos & Other Poems (1878)
Ultima Thule (1880)
In the Harbor (1882)
Michel Angelo: A Fragment (incomplete; published posthumously)

Translations

Coplas de Don Jorge Manrique (Translation from Spanish) (1833)
Dante's Divine Comedy (Translation) (1867)

Anthologies

Poets and Poetry of Europe (Translations) (1845)
The Waif (1845)
Poems of Places (1874)